The 'Southern' Accent 'cajun & creole Cookbook ★

Elena Embrioni & Frances Wood

Moulin

Moulin Publishing Limited
P. O. Box #560
Norval, Ontario
Canada   L0P 1K0

First Edition

Canadian Cataloguing in Publication Data

Wood, Frances
The Southern Accent Cajun and Creole Cookbook

Includes index.
ISBN 0-9697079-7-5

1. Cookery, Creole. 2. Cookery, Cajun. 3. Cookery, American—Louisiana style. I. Embrioni, Elena II. Title.

Tx715.W568 1966   641.59763   C96-900474-5

Photographs by Ellen Rehak and Frances Wood.
Painting on back cover: "Southern Serenade" by Robin Grindley. Copyright © 1996 by Robin Grindley.
Used by permission.

Cover and interior design by Richard Bingham
Typesetting by Heidy Lawrance Associates

Contents

Acknowledgements

All our staff are people hand-picked from diverse cultural backgrounds and interests and who work together to create a style and ambiance that starts in the kitchen and carries to the front – something that has been greatly appreciated by the owners and customers alike.

Special thanks to my staff for their support to make this cookbook happen – after many years of procrastination.

Elena Embrioni is an essential part of this accomplishment. Congratulations Elena! With the support of many characters in the kitchen – we did it.

Thank you to Ed Boyce, my publisher, for the gentle nagging and getting the ball rolling. And thanks to all the crew at Moulin Publishing.

Special mention for music suggestions to Richard Crouse. Thanks to Karen Scarth, an old employee, for the typeface – Soupbone. Thanks to Richard Bingham for a great design. Thanks to Ellen Rehak for the photographs, to Neil Huber for his patience and work on the computer; to my partner Robin Grindley who's artwork appears in the book and on the walls of our restaurant; to Paul Madaule for his support – without it, the restaurant would not have come to be; and last but not least to Billy Munnelly who introduced me to the restaurant business and has continued to be my mentor. And there are probably many more people to thank, but my space is limited so –

Thanks y'all!

About the Southern Accent Restaurant and Bar

When I first arrived in Canada from Ireland in the mid 1960s, I worked as a registered nurse, but it wasn't until the late 1970s that my good friends Billy Munnelly and Geraldine and Rosaleen Charleton convinced me to turn in my bed pans for bus pans. We opened the Rosedale Diner and I was hooked!

After a couple of years, Billy moved to Stratford. Dubie Filar of By the Way Cafe fame became the new owner and we became partners. It was after Dubie spiked my food with hot peppers that I developed my taste for spicier food. It was also during this time that I met Robin Grindley who had a real "knack for the wack." His one liners became famous in Rosedale and people would come by not only for the food but just to talk to him. We developed a great rapport so when I was ready to move on, to start something of my own, it was natural for Robin to eventually join me.

We named the restaurant Southern Accent knowing that I wanted to serve spicy food from the south but I didn't yet know that Cajun and Creole cooking would be our focus. I did know that I wanted a place where all my interests – folk art, antiques, music and food – could be brought together.

My first Cajun experience was at The Great Jones Cafe in New York. I was lured by a small sign in the window offering "Cajun Martinis." The restaurant was alive with strange music which sounded very Irish, except that it was too happy, and the room was filled with a delicious aroma of Jambalaya. This was to be the start of my wonderful and passionate relationship with Louisiana cooking. Of course, the martini helped – ice cold with that warm spicy feeling in my throat. It was all too good to be true.

I returned to Toronto, armed with what I considered to be the ingredients for a unique restaurant: good food, wonderful music, ambiance and fun. All the things New Orleans epitomizes to an excess!

To find out more about Cajun and Creole cooking I bought Paul Prudhomme's book, *Louisiana Kitchen*, which proved to be invaluable. But, there's nothing like the "hands-on" approach, so I wrote to Commander's Palace and Paul Prudhomme at K-Paul's Louisiana Kitchen, two restaurants in New Orleans, to ask them if they'd allow me and the staff at Southern Accent to come and observe them in their kitchens. It was the very best idea we'd had.

While in Louisiana we visited several restaurants which not only imparted their secrets to us, but also invited us to "come back tomorrow and work with the cook." At a restaurant called Frankie and Johnny's I made a gumbo, step by step – a method we still follow faithfully. Our trip to New Orleans turned out to be a great success and would be the first of many.

Since then, we have had a succession of chefs who have each added a little *Lagniappe* – an old Creole word meaning something special or extra – to our menus. David Duffield, the residing chef in 1988, was the first chef who was really in tune to my ideas. We always worked together, exploring Louisiana and confirming that our direction was worthwhile.

In 1990 Elena Embrioni walked through the door of Southern Accent to answer an ad for a prep-cook. She possessed little English but had a great willingness to work hard and a genuine interest in food. I recognized in her a kindred spirit, and I was proven right! With her enthusiasm and eagerness to learn, she observed everyone in the kitchen and watched the resident chef carefully. Then one day there was an opening in the kitchen and Elena stepped in.

Elena moved to Canada from Argentina, where she'd worked in a professional kitchen and discovered her destiny, "cooking from the heart!" She soon became obsessed with the Cajun and Creole food at the restaurant, which so resembled what she had cooked at home. For the past five years she has been in charge of the kitchen – to the great approval of all.

Elena has been influenced by many other cuisines and has borrowed from them to add to our Cajun and Creole fare at the restaurant. The result is this wonderful and innovative collection of recipes, along with our version of the traditional ones. I hope these recipes don't keep you from coming to see us, after all, we all need to get out of the kitchen some time!

Frances Wood
Southern Accent, Toronto

What is Louisiana cooking?

For Louisiana cooking, take one part classical French cuisine and combine it with equal parts of Spanish and Anglo-Saxon cooking. Blend well with the herbs and spices from France and Spain – coupled with seasoning influences of the Choctaws and Chickasaws. Then add to this the ingenuity of the Acadian (Cajun) refugees, who had to learn the use of nature's own foods wherever they were to be found. And whose ingenuity gave us Jambalaya, court bouillon, red beans and rice, grits, grillades, pain-perdu, coush-coush caille, and gumbo. Add to all of this the exotic taste and magic seasoning powers of the African cook, and, in later years, that of the Italians, Haitians and Yugoslavians.

Voila! We have Louisiana cookery whose tenets are economy and simplicity governed by patience and skill all combined to produce a subtle, exotic, and succulent cuisine recognized throughout the world.

What's the difference between Cajun and Creole cooking?

Cajun cooking is similar to Creole cookery in many ways, but with more spices, more herbs, more hot peppers and more gusto. The best way to distinguish them is to describe Creole as sophisticated city cooking and Cajun as country cooking – less inhibited and more daring, slapdash, and inventive.

Getting Started

The Tools

Knives: The most important tools in your kitchen should be a good set of sharp knives. Keep a sharpening stone on hand so that your knives are always ready to use.

Pots and Pans: A good set of pots and pans are an excellent investment for anyone interested in cooking. It's helpful to have a variety of shapes and sizes that allow you to work on more than one part of your recipe at a time. Some European lines, such as *Le Creuset*, are cast iron coated with porcelain and are excellent for this style of cooking. Also, keep in mind that different pots and pans have different uses.

A good quality cast iron pan is the only pan that should be used for blackening and one should be kept aside for this purpose.

Our favourite all-purpose pan is a copper-lined stainless steel one that is best for holding heat and distributing it evenly. An electric deep-fryer and a deep skillet are helpful – be sure that the thermostats are accurate.

Peppermills: A great deal of pepper is used in Louisiana cooking and there's nothing like freshly ground pepper. Try and keep one mill for white pepper and one for black.

Miscellaneous essentials: Keep a variety of inexpensive wooden spoons and spatulas, tongs, wire whisks and a good pair of long oven mitts.

The Spice Shelf

The quality of your spices are important because they provide much of the flavour of Cajun and Creole cooking. Dried spices are used the most, so keep an eye on your selection to ensure that they are still fresh. Check your spices fairly regularly. If their aroma is faint, throw them away and buy fresh ones. Stale spices leave a slightly bitter taste. If the colour of your cayenne or paprika changes, don't even bother to use it.

Peppers: The most widely used peppers are powdered cayenne and liquid cayenne, crushed chilies, chili powder, chili flakes, black peppercorns, white peppercorns and Spanish paprika.

Herbs and Spices: Here are some dried herbs and spices to have on hand. You'll probably have most of them already. Whole bay leaves, dried thyme, oregano, caraway seeds, rosemary leaves, marjoram, ground mace, whole cloves, whole allspice, ground allspice, nutmeg, ground mustard, gumbo file, cumin, cinnamon and creme of tartar.

Occasionally these ingredients are used as well: chopped chives, sweet basil, chervil, sage, turmeric, saffron, whole dill seed, caraway seeds, celery seed, anise seed, dried ground chicory, balsamic vinegar and capers.

Basic Mixtures: One way to make cooking Cajun and Creole easy is by keeping some of these basic mixtures on hand. These include blackening spices, bronzing spices, crab and shrimp boil spices. The recipes for these mixtures can be found in the *Lagniappe*. Also, try and keep on hand Worcestershire sauce, olive oil, orange peels, Tabasco sauce and Creole mustard.

Once your pantry is set, pick a tune (see Discography) and start cooking.

Breads

Hush Puppies/2

Jalapeno Corn Bread/3

Pain Perdu /4

Feta Olive Bread /5

Rosemary Flat Bread /6

Hush Puppies

MAKES 2 DOZEN

Hush puppies, the sweetheart of fried catfish, are said to have got their name in the ante-bellum days. In summertime, slaves cooked their meals over an outdoor fire. Overcome by the delicious smells rising from the skillet, the family dog would walk around whining. To quiet the dog down, the cook would toss him a delicious tid-bit and say, "Hush, puppy!" In the restaurant we serve them as a side bread dish.

Ingredients

1 1/4 cups sifted, all purpose flour (300 mL)
3/4 cup yellow cornmeal (150 mL)
1 tsp salt (5 mL)
1/2 tbsp white pepper (7 mL)
2 eggs
1 10-oz (300-g) can creamed corn
4 tbsp milk (50 mL)
1 1/2 tbsp olive oil (20 mL)
1/4 cup jalapeno peppers, seeded and chopped (50 mL)
1/2 cup onions, chopped (100 mL)
oil for deep-frying

Directions

1. Heat oil in a deep-fryer to 350°F (180°C). See Lagniappe for tips on deep-frying.
2. Combine dry ingredients with a fork.
3. In a separate bowl, combine eggs, corn, milk and olive oil, and whip.
4. Add peppers and onions to the above, and mix well. If you'd like a hotter mixture add some seeds from the jalapeno pepper to the batter.
5. Fold the wet mixture into the dry mixture.
6. Using a wet teaspoon, drop the batter by spoonfulls into the hot oil.
7. After about 1 minute, flip and allow to cook for 1 more minute, until they rise and are golden brown.
8. Drain on a paper towel to remove excess oil. Serve hot.

Jalapeno Corn Bread

SERVES EIGHT

This is a great Southern staple bread. There are so many variations. We add jalapenos to spice it up and then drizzle it with honey just before serving. You can omit the jalapenos if you wish.

Directions

1. In a large bowl, combine flour, cornmeal, sugar, baking powder, salt and jalapenos until there are no lumps.
2. In a smaller bowl whisk together milk, shortening and eggs until frothy.
3. Add liquid ingredients to dry ingredients and fold.
4. Pour the mixture into a greased 8" x 8" (20 cm x 20 cm) pan, and bake in a preheated oven at 350°F (180°C) for about 30 minutes, or until golden brown.
5. Remove pan from oven, leave cake in pan, and allow to cool on rack.
6. Remove the cooled cornbread from the pan, cut into 2½" x 2½" (6 cm x 6 cm) squares and drizzle each square with about 2 tbsp (30 mL) of honey. Serve immediately.

Ingredients

1 1/3 cups all-purpose flour (320 mL)
1 1/3 cups yellow cornmeal (320 mL)
2/3 cup sugar (150 mL)
5 tsp baking powder (25 mL)
1/2 tsp salt (2 mL)
1/2 cup jalapenos, chopped and seeded (120 mL)
1 1/4 cups milk (300 mL)
5 tbsp shortening, melted (75 mL)
2 eggs, lightly beaten
1 cup liquid honey (240 mL)

Pain Perdu

This version of French toast originated as a way of using up leftover, stale bread.
We like it so much that we buy extra French bread and set it on the kitchen counter to get stale.

Ingredients

6 eggs
2 cups sugar (480 mL)
1/2 tsp cinnamon (2 mL)
1/2 tsp nutmeg (2 mL)
3 cups milk (3/4 L)
3 tbsp vanilla extract (45 mL)
1/2 cup orange juice (120 mL)
1 1/2 tbsp grated orange rind (22 mL)
1 1/2 tbsp lemon rind (22 mL)
1 cup oil (240 mL)
1 loaf stale French bread
confectioners' sugar
maple syrup

Directions

1. Beat together eggs, sugar, cinnamon and nutmeg. Then add the milk, vanilla extract, orange juice, lemon and orange rinds, and mix well.
2. Slice bread into 12 1" (2.5 cm) slices, on an angle.
3. Heat oil to 300°F (150°C). Dip slices of bread into the egg mixture and let soak for about 1 minute.
4. Place dipped bread in pan and cook until lightly browned and crispy on both sides. Remove from pan to paper towels to remove excess oil. Keep warm in a low oven until all the slices have been cooked.
5. Sprinkle the pain perdu with confectioners' sugar and serve with maple syrup and fresh berries.

Feta Olive Bread

This is Frances' favourite bread. She likes to have a couple of pieces with almost every meal, especially with our Tomato-Pernod soup. We use foccacia bread in the restaurant because it's made with olive oil and herbs that nicely complement the feta cheese.

Directions

1. Put olive pieces into food processor, and pulse twice or until they resemble coarse bread crumbs.
2. Add butter and feta cheese and pulse twice.
3. Add garlic purée and pepper, and pulse once.
4. Smear this mixture onto the bread slices and bake under broiler for 5 minutes, or until cheese bubbles.

This mixture can be kept in the refrigerator, covered tightly, for up to 3 months.

Ingredients

4 oz black olives, chopped (114 g)
4 oz butter, softened (114 g)
1/4 lb feta cheese, cubed (114 g)
1/2 tsp garlic purée (2.5 mL)
1 tsp black pepper (5 mL)
1 French stick, cut in slices

Rosemary Flat Bread

SERVES SIX TO EIGHT

*We created this recipe to accompany a Blackened Leg of Lamb
that was served at the 1995 Feast of the Fields. We liked it so much that we
continue to have it as an occasional weekly special. It can also be served
cut into wedges with a fun salad or soup.*

Ingredients

2 packages active dry yeast
1 tbsp granulated sugar (15 mL)
2 tsp salt (10 mL)
1 1/2 cups warm water (360 mL)
3 1/2 cups all-purpose flour (865 mL)
1/4 cup olive oil (60 mL)
1 egg
1 tbsp fresh rosemary, chopped (15 mL)
1 egg white beaten with 1 tbsp
(15 mL) water

Directions

1. In a large mixing bowl combine yeast, sugar and salt. Add ¼ cup (60 mL) of water.
2. Beat mixture for 3 minutes with a wooden spoon.
3. Add ½ cup (120 mL) of the flour and continue beating for 2 or 3 minutes.
4. Alternately add 1 cup (240 mL) of the flour and ½ cup (120 mL) of the water to make a fairly soft dough, reserving about ½ cup (120 mL) flour for kneading.
5. Remove dough to a floured surface and knead for several minutes until it springs back very quickly when you press your fingers into the dough, which must be smooth and satiny, and all the flour should be absorbed.

Continued…

6. Let the dough rest, covered with a towel, for about 15 minutes, then cut it into three equal pieces.
7. Rest the dough again for 10 to 15 minutes.
8. Using the palms of your hands, roll out each piece ¼" (0.6 cm) thick and as large as the baking sheet you will use.
9. Oil or butter the baking sheet, sprinkle lightly with rosemary, and place dough on sheets.
10. Let sit 20 minutes, until they just barely begin to rise.
11. Just before putting them in the oven, brush with the egg and water mixture.
12. Bake in a slow oven at 300°F (150°C) for about 30 minutes, until nicely browned.

Variation

The same recipe can be used to make bread sticks. Omit the rosemary, and in step 6 cut the dough into nine pieces instead of three. After you've let the dough rest make 1" (2.5 cm) rolls, and follow the rest of the steps.

Soups

Chicken, Duck or Beef Stock/10

Fish Stock/11

Vegetable Stock/12

Creole Onion Soup/13

Okra Meat Gumbo/14

Yam Soup/16

Wa-Hoo Roasted Sweet Corn Chowder/17

Black-Eyed Pea Soup/18

Linda's Peanut Soup/19

Organic Apple Cider and Red Lentil Soup/20

Tomato Pernod Soup/21

Watermelon Gazpacho/22

Chicken, Duck or Beef Stock

MAKES 3 QUARTS (3 L)

Nothing can take the place of homemade stock. Oven roasting the bones first adds extra flavour — the New Orleans way!

Ingredients

2 lbs raw poultry or beef bones, remove skin and fat (2 kg)

1 tbsp olive oil (15 mL)

1 large onion, peeled and sliced

1 carrot, peeled and chopped

1 celery stalk, chopped

1 whole garlic head, cut in half

2 bay leaves

1/2 tsp black peppercorns (2.5 mL)

1 sprig of fresh thyme

1 sprig of fresh basil

4 quarts cold water (4 L)

Directions

1. Preheat oven to 425°F (218°C). Place bones in a roasting pan, drizzle with olive oil and roast for 15 minutes until browned.
2. Transfer bones to a stock-pot, add vegetables, seasonings and water to cover.
3. On high heat bring liquid to a boil, then reduce heat, cover and simmer for about 1½ hours.
4. Remove from heat and immediately immerse pot in a sink of ice water to reduce any bacteria growth.
5. When cool, refrigerate stock.
6. The following day, skim off the fat when it has solidified.

Fish Stock

Makes 2 quarts (2 L)

Ask your fish store owner to give you heads and bones. At the restaurant we also include all our shrimp shells.

Directions

1. In a stock-pot on high heat, combine all the ingredients and cover with water.
2. Bring to boil and reduce heat to simmer for 30 to 40 minutes.
3. For a rich stock, continue to reduce stock and add water.
4. Remove from heat and immerse pot in a sink of ice water to reduce any bacteria growth.
5. When cool, refrigerate stock.
6. The following day, skim away any impurities and fat that have risen to the surface.

Ingredients

2 lbs fish bones and heads
(no skin or fat) (1 kg)
shrimp shells
1 onion, peeled and halved
1 carrot, chopped
1 celery stalk, chopped
1 head garlic, chopped
1/2 tsp black peppercorns (2.5 mL)
2 bay leaves
1 sprig of thyme
1 sprig of basil
3 quarts cold water (3 L)

Vegetable Stock

MAKES 2 QUARTS (2 L)

Refrigerate or freeze your stock in 2- to 4-cup containers or ice-cube trays for use in individual dishes.

Ingredients

1 leek, chopped
1 tbsp vegetable oil (15 mL)
1 medium-large onion, peeled and sliced
1 celery stalk, chopped
1 carrot, peeled and chopped
2 heads garlic, halved
4 quarts cold water (4 L)
1 green pepper, seeded and chopped
1 tomato, coarsely chopped
2 ears of corn, kernels removed
and saved
1/2 lb mushroom stems, rinsed and
trimmed (129 g)
6 bay leaves
1 tsp fresh thyme, chopped (5 mL)
1 tsp fresh basil, chopped (5 mL)
1 tsp fresh oregano, chopped (5 mL)
1 tsp fresh parsley, chopped (5 mL)
1/3 tsp whole peppercorns (1.5 mL)

Directions

1. Heat the oil in a large stock-pot over high heat.
2. Add the onions, carrots, celery and garlic, and sauté, stirring occasionally until the onions are translucent (approximately 3 to 4 minutes).
3. Add the remaining ingredients, and bring to a boil.
4. Reduce the heat to low and simmer, uncovered for about 1 hour and 45 minutes.
5. Remove from heat, strain the stock, and immerse pot in a sink of ice water to reduce any bacteria growth. Let cool and refrigerate.
6. The following day, skim away any impurities that have risen to the surface.

Creole Onion Soup

The old Creole cooks were almost unanimous in their opinions that the best soup produced in their kitchens was onion. This is one of those refreshing dishes composed of honest tastes.

Directions

1. Melt butter in a heavy saucepan and sauté sliced onions.
2. When onions are golden brown, slowly add seasonings and flour, and cook for 1 minute.
3. Add stock, bay leaf, wine, stir and simmer 15 minutes.
4. Add salt to taste and correct seasoning if necessary.
5. Serve with a crouton of toasted French bread topped with melted Monterey Jack cheese.

Ingredients

2 tbsp butter (30 mL)
1 1/2 medium onions, thinly sliced
2 tbsp all-purpose flour (30 mL)
8 cups chicken stock (2 L)
1 small bay leaf
1/2 cup dry white wine (120 mL)
2 tsp blackening spice (page 125) (10 mL)
salt to taste
toasted croutons
Monterey Jack cheese for melting

Okra Meat Gumbo

We could not open the restaurant doors without a Gumbo. Gumbo can be refrigerated and will keep well — some say it's even better the next day. For more information on making roux see the Lagniappe.
Gumbo is a New Orleans favourite and a staple dish that has many variations. It's an improvisational dish — this is our version.

Seasoning Ingredients

2 bay leaves
1 1/2 tsp salt (7.5 mL)
1/2 tsp paprika (2.5 mL)
1/2 tsp cayenne (2.5 mL)
1/2 tsp white pepper (2.5 mL)
1/2 tsp black pepper (2.5 mL)
1/2 tsp thyme (2.5 mL)
1/4 tsp oregano (1.25 mL)

Making the Gumbo

1. Combine and sift together the seasonings.
2. In a large saucepan, heat half of the butter and half of the oil.
3. Add the onion, celery and green pepper and sauté and set aside.
4. At the same time, place Andouille and ham into a baking dish.
5. In a second baking pan, place the okra mixed with remaining butter cut into pieces.
6. Place both these pans in a preheated oven at 350°F (180°C) and roast approximately 15 minutes, until meat and vegetables are browned.
7. In a large pot heat the chicken stock to a boil on a high heat.
8. In a skillet, heat remaining oil to smoking. Add the flour.

Continued…

9. Using a whisk, work the oil and flour into a light brown roux. Be sure to wear oven mitts for protection because this very hot mixture can splash.
10. Remove from heat, add green onion, garlic and seasonings, and combine well.
11. Add heated stock to the saucepan with onion and celery and bring to a boil.
12. To this, add the roasted meat and cook a further 10 minutes.
13. Add roux mixture and reduce to a thicker consistency – about 5 to 10 minutes.
14. Add poultry when gumbo is almost ready and then add okra. Cook for about 5 minutes, or until poultry is cooked, to further blend flavours.
15. Add fresh herbs in large amounts, skim off fat and serve with the rice of your choice.
16. Sprinkle with file powder if desired.

Soup Ingredients

1 1/2 tbsp butter (22 mL)
1/2 cup vegetable oil (120 mL)
1 cup onion, chopped (240 mL)
1/2 cup celery, chopped (120 mL)
1/2 cup green pepper, chopped (120 mL)
1 3/4 cup okra, cut into 3/4" (1.5 cm) pieces (420 mL)
1 Andouille sausage (or another smoked sausage) cut into 1 1/2" (4 cm) disks
6 oz Black Forest ham, cut into cubes (168 g)
10 cups chicken stock (2.5 L)
1/4 cup flour (60 mL)
1/2 cup green onion, chopped (120 mL)
1 tbsp garlic (15 mL)
2 cups roasted poultry, cubed (duck, chicken, turkey) (480 mL)
fresh basil, or other fresh herbs
file powder to sprinkle on top (optional)

Yam Soup

Elena loves yams so she tries to always have something on the menu that includes them. This is the comfort food to make on a cold winter day.

Ingredients

4 large yams, peeled and quartered
1/4 lb butter (114 g)
1 cup onions, finely chopped (240 mL)
1 tsp garlic (5 mL)
1 tsp nutmeg (5 mL)
1/2 tsp cinnamon (2.5 mL)
2 tsp cayenne (10 mL)
1/2 cup brown sugar (120 mL)
8 cups hot vegetable stock (page 12) (2 L)
1 cup whipping cream
(35% fat) (240 mL)

Directions

1. Bake yams at 400°F (200°C) until tender.
2. Melt butter in a saucepan and add onions.
3. Cook onions until golden brown, approximately 10 minutes, on high heat.
4. Add garlic and cook 4 minutes.
5. Add nutmeg, cinnamon, cayenne, and brown sugar, and cook 1 minute.
6. Add yams, and cook for 3 to 4 minutes, mashing them in the pan.
7. Add the vegetable stock and cook for 30 minutes, adding more stock if needed. Be sure to break up any large lumps of yam with a masher.
8. Add cream, bring soup to a boil and remove from heat.
9. Correct seasoning if necessary, and serve.

Wa-Hoo Roasted Sweet Corn Chowder

SERVES SIX TO EIGHT

This name came about after someone tried this soup and said, "Ya-hoo, this is hot, hot, hot!"
We heard "Wa-hoo!" and the name stuck.

Directions

1. Roast the fresh corn and jalapeno in the oven at 350°F (180°C) for 45 minutes. The corn will have a golden colour when it's done.
2. Cut the corn from the cob. Seed and chop the jalapeno pepper.
3. In a pot on medium heat, sauté onions, red and green peppers, garlic and spices in butter.
4. Add creamed corn, fresh corn, milk, roasted chopped jalapeno, and let simmer for 15 minutes.
5. Remove from heat, add coriander and salt to taste if necessary.
6. Serve immediately.

Ingredients

2 cobs fresh corn, husk off

1 jalapeno pepper, whole

1/4 cup onion, finely chopped (60 mL)

1/4 cup green pepper, finely chopped (60 mL)

1/4 cup red pepper, finely chopped (60 mL)

3 1/2 cups canned creamed corn (840 mL)

1 tbsp fresh coriander (30 mL)

2 tbsp roasted garlic, chopped (30 mL)

3 cups milk (720 mL)

1/2 tsp cayenne (2.5 mL)

1/4 tsp cumin (1.25 mL)

2 tbsp butter (30 mL)

salt and pepper to taste

Black-Eyed Pea Soup

SERVES SIX TO EIGHT

Talk about comfort food! The African influence on Cajun cuisine was indeed a comfort to all.
This is a nice wintertime soup — a must try.

Ingredients

3 cups black-eyed peas (720 mL)
1 cup onions, chopped (240 mL)
1 cup celery, chopped (240 mL)
1 cup green pepper, chopped (240 mL)
1/4 lb butter (114 g)
1/8 cup olive oil (29 mL)
1 tbsp garlic (15 mL)
1 tsp cumin (5 mL)
1 tsp chili powder (5 mL)
1 tsp chili flakes (5 mL)
8 cups vegetable stock (page 12) (2 L)
blackened tomato salsa (page 35)

Directions

1. Cook black-eyed peas in water until soft, strain and rinse in cold water.
2. Sauté vegetables in butter and olive oil on high until they become golden brown.
3. Add garlic and sauté 3 minutes more.
4. Add spices and sauté for 1 minute.
5. Add peas and stir to combine all ingredients, approximately 2 minutes.
6. Add 8 cups (2 L) of stock and allow to cook for 30 minutes, adding more stock if needed.
7. Purée liquid in a food processor and return to heat.
8. Correct seasonings and serve with blackened tomato salsa.

Linda's Peanut Soup

SERVES EIGHT TO TEN

One day Linda, one of our cooks, came to work and told us she was going to make a peanut soup. We all thought she had lost her mind, but she surprised us all and created a soup everybody loved.

Directions

1. Sauté onions in oil until translucent, add garlic, and cook for 5 minutes.
2. Add coriander seeds, cumin seeds and chili flakes, and cook a further 5 minutes.
3. Add peanut butter, coconut milk and Tahini, mix well and simmer for 5 minutes or until the mixture has a smooth texture. Tahini can be purchased in most grocery or health food stores.
4. Add hot chicken stock, bring to a boil, and simmer for 20 minutes, stirring frequently. Add more chicken stock if consistency is too thick.
5. When ready to serve, add cream, and slowly bring to a boil, stirring constantly. Don't worry the cream won't curdle.

Ingredients

1/4 cup vegetable oil (60 mL)
1 cup onion, chopped (240 mL)
1 tbsp garlic (15 mL)
1 tbsp coriander seed (15 mL)
1 tbsp cumin seeds (15 mL)
1 tbsp chili flakes (15 mL)
1 1/2 cup peanut butter (360 mL)
2 cups coconut milk (480 mL)
1/2 cup Tahini sauce (120 mL)
6 cups hot chicken stock (1.5 L)
1 cup whipping cream
(35% fat) (240 mL)
salt to taste

Organic Apple Cider and Red Lentil Soup

Organic apple cider is less sweet than conventional ciders, and can be purchased at most health-food stores or organic farmer's markets. A visiting chef from our organic lunch gave us the idea, and when Elena tasted the apple cider from the South Bay vineyards the recipe was born!

Ingredients

1/2 cup leeks, chopped (120 mL)
1 cup onions, chopped (240 mL)
1/4 cup olive oil (60 mL)
2 cups red lentils, dry (480 mL)
1 tsp mace (5 mL)
3/4 tbsp chili flakes (12 mL)
2 tbsp minced ginger (30 mL)
8 cups organic apple cider (2 L)
salt to taste

Directions

1. Sauté leeks and onions in olive oil over medium heat until they're transparent.
2. Add garlic and cook another 5 minutes.
3. Add lentils, mace, chili flakes, and ginger, and cook for 5 minutes.
4. Add cider, and cook until lentils are tender, about 15 minutes.
5. Serve with a dollop of yogurt.

Tomato Pernod Soup

SERVES SIX TO EIGHT

This recipe came with us from the Rosedale Diner days. I still believe it is a wonderful and very easy soup to do — so easy, Elena says even I can do it! You will still see it occasionally on our menu. We serve it with grilled blackened shrimps or scallops.

Directions

1. Heat butter over medium heat. Add onions, garlic, and seasonings, and sauté until onions are transparent.
2. In a separate saucepan, heat cream until nearly boiling.
3. Add tomatoes to onion mixture. Heat to boil, then reduce heat immediately to medium-low.
4. Add heated cream to tomato sauce, add tomato paste, and continue to simmer for 15 minutes.
5. Season to taste and add Pernod.

Ingredients

2 tbsp butter (30 mL)

1 large onion, chopped

1 tsp garlic, chopped (5 mL)

2 tbsp dried oregano (10 mL)

2 tbsp dried basil (10 mL)

1 tsp black pepper (5 mL)

1/2 tsp crushed chilies (2.5 mL)

6 cups canned tomatoes, puréed (1.5 L)

3 cups whipping cream (35% fat) (360 mL)

1 tbsp tomato paste (5 mL)

1 oz Pernod (30 mL)

salt and pepper to taste

Watermelon Gazpacho

This summertime soup is a nice alternative to traditional gazpacho. Make sure you get a good watermelon. The ends of the watermelon should be yellow and soft to the touch, and it should sound hollow when tapped.

Ingredients

1/2 watermelon
1 purple onion
1 cucumber
1 red pepper
1 jalapeno pepper
cayenne, salt and pepper to taste

Directions

1. Remove seeds from watermelon, cut into chunks and purée in a food processor until smooth.
2. Finely chop the onion, red pepper and jalapeno.
3. Remove the skin and seeds from cucumber and chop into cubes.
4. In a large bowl combine watermelon and vegetables.
5. Add seasonings to taste
6. Chill for about 2 hours and serve.

Salads

Zydeco Green Salad with Balsamic Soya Vinaigrette/24

Arugula Salad with Pancetta and Andouille Warm Vinaigrette/25

Caesar Salad and Cajun Croutons and Andouille Bits/26

Mixed Bean Salad/27

Pasta Salad/28

Potato Salad/29

Tangerine Vinaigrette/30

Wild Mushroom Vinaigrette/31

Zydeco Green Salad with Balsamic Soya Vinaigrette

SERVES TWELVE

At the restaurant we serve this salad as our house salad.

Ingredients

1 1/4 cups Soya sauce,
light Kikoman (300 mL)

1 1/4 cup balsamic vinegar (300 mL)

1 cup olive oil, light (240 mL)

2 pinches salt

2 pinches pepper

mixed organic greens with some radicchio,
watercress and leaf lettuce

Directions

1. Combine soya sauce and vinegar in a bowl with a whisk.
2. Slowly add olive oil, until emulsified.
3. Add salt and pepper to taste.
4. Wash the salad greens and pat dry. Serve with 1 oz (30 mL) dressing per person.

Arugula Salad with Pancetta and Andouille Warm Vinaigrette

SERVES TEN TO TWELVE

*We always have a Creole salad special and this particular one is a favourite with our customers.
For a variation on this salad reheat the vinaigrette in a microwave oven for 1 minute, or in a saucepan, until warm but
not hot, and serve with steamed new potatoes on top of the arugula.*

Directions

1. Heat 2 tbsp (30 mL) of olive oil in a saucepan, and add pancetta and Andouille.
2. Turn the heat to low and let the meat crisp.
3. Remove some of the fat and add the onions, sauté until translucent.
4. Transfer mixture to a bowl, add vinegars and whisk.
5. Slowly add olive oil, still whisking, until the vinaigrette becomes thick.
6. On a large 9" (22.5 cm) plate, arrange the arugula leaves in a wheel and drizzle with approximately 1 oz (30 mL) of dressing. Serve immediately.

Ingredients

2 tbsp olive oil (30 mL)
6 slices of pancetta, chopped
1 Andouille, chopped
1/2 cup onion, chopped (120 mL)
1/4 cup balsamic vinegar (60 mL)
1/4 cup red wine vinegar (60 mL)
1 cup olive oil (240 mL)
salt and pepper to taste
1 bunch of baby arugula per person, washed

Caesar Salad with Cajun Croutons and Andouille Bits

SERVES FOUR TO SIX

Chef Elena only eats Caesar salad in our restaurant. Try this version and you'll understand why.

Dressing Ingredients

2 tbsp garlic (30 mL)
1 1/2 tbsp capers (22.5 mL)
3 anchovy pieces
2 tbsp Creole mustard (30 mL)
1 whole egg
1/3 cup vegetable oil (80 mL)
1 cup olive oil (240 mL)
1/4 cup red wine vinegar (60 mL)
1 tbsp balsamic vinegar (15 mL)
1 tbsp lemon juice (15 mL)
2 tbsp parmesan cheese (30 mL)
salt and pepper to taste
1/2 head of Romaine lettuce per person

Crouton Ingredients

1/2 French stick, cubed
1/2 stick butter
1/2 tsp blackening mix (see Lagniappe) (2.5 mL)

The Bits

1 Andouille sausage, cut into bits

Making the Dressing...

1. In a food processor, purée garlic, capers and anchovies.
2. Add mustard and egg, and pulse 3 times.
3. Slowly add oils until emulsified.
4. Remove mixture from machine; add vinegars, lemon juice and cheese, and whisk.
5. Add salt and pepper to taste, and set aside.
6. Wash and pat dry lettuce, and break leaves by hand.
7. Add 1 oz (30 mL) of dressing per person, toss gently and add toasted croutons and Andouille bits.

the Croutons...

1. In a pan, heat butter, add blackening mix and cook for 1 minute.
2. Add the cubed bread, toss well, then bake in the oven for 10 minutes at 350°F (180°C).

...and the Andouille bits

1. Put Andouille bits in a baking dish and cook for 20 minutes at 350°F (180°C), stirring periodically.

Mixed Bean Salad

SERVES SIX TO EIGHT

A great summertime salad, to cool you off on those hot nights.

Directions

1. Soak black-eyed peas, black beans (not green beans) and chick peas overnight in cold water.
2. Drain and put into a pot with fresh water.
3. Bring to a boil and let simmer until tender.
4. Remove from the pot and drain.
5. Boil green beans until al dente and drain.
6. Put all beans and peas into a bowl with the remaining ingredients and let sit for 2 hours.
7. Refrigerate until chilled before serving.

Ingredients

1/4 cup black-eyed peas, dry (60 mL)

1/4 cup black beans, dry (60 mL)

1/4 cup chick peas, dry (60 mL)

1 cup green beans (240 mL)

1/2 cup red pepper, chopped (120 mL)

1/4 cup coriander, chopped (60 mL)

1/2 cup green onions, chopped (120 mL)

1/3 cup purple onions, chopped (80 mL)

1/4 cup balsamic vinegar (60 mL)

1/2 cup olive oil (120 mL)

salt and pepper to taste

Pasta Salad

SERVES TEN

Great for those backyard summer barbecues. We always have this salad on our buffet menus and summer boat cruises on Lake Ontario.

Ingredients

4 cups cooked rigatoni, fusilli,
ziti or penne (1 kg)

1/3 cup pitted black olives, halved (80 mL)

1/3 cup pimento–stuffed green olives,
halved (80 mL)

1/4 cup green onions, chopped (60 mL)

1 cup tomatoes, peeled and
chopped (240 mL)

1 tbsp oregano, dry (15 mL)

1 tsp minced garlic (5 mL)

1/4 tsp salt (1.25 mL)

4 turns freshly ground pepper

3 tbsp olive oil (45 mL)

1 cup coarse feta cheese (240 mL)

Directions

1. Toss all ingredients together in a bowl until thoroughly blended. Serve immediately or store overnight in an air-tight container in the refrigerator.

Potato Salad

SERVES SIX TO EIGHT

It wouldn't be right not to have this dish when you are doing a southern meal.

Directions

1. Boil potatoes until fork-tender.
2. Drain potatoes and return to pot on low heat with no water, for just a few minutes.
3. Mix all ingredients in a bowl and let sit for at least 1 hour before serving. Cover well and store in the refrigerator.

Ingredients

6 medium Yukon Gold potatoes, cubed

1/4 cup purple onion, chopped (60 mL)

1 tsp garlic, minced (5 mL)

1/4 cup hot sauce (60 mL)

1/2 cup basic mayonnaise
(see Lagniappe) (120 mL)

1 tsp cayenne (5 mL)

1/8 cup green onion, chopped (40 mL)

1/4 cup roasted red pepper (60 mL)

2 celery stalks, chopped

1 tbsp fresh basil, chopped (15 mL)

salt and pepper to taste

Tangerine Vinaigrette

MAKES 1 ⅓ (325 mL) CUPS

Ingredients

1 1/2 oz tangerine, clementine or orange
juice (45 mL)

1 1/2 oz red wine vinegar (45 mL)

1/2 oz walnut oil (15 mL)

4 1/4 oz vegetable oil (128 mL)

salt to taste

1 tsp black pepper (5 mL)

1 tsp fresh basil (5 mL)

pinch dry tarragon

zest of 1/2 orange, clementine or mandarin

1 tsp Creole mustard (5 mL)

Directions

1. Combine the juice, vinegar, mustard and pepper.
2. Gradually add the walnut and vegetable oils while whisking constantly.
3. Add herbs, zest, mustard and salt. All these steps should be done quickly, lasting 15 minutes.

NOTE: Because of the citrus, this dressing cannot be kept longer than 3 days.

Wild Mushroom Vinaigrette

MAKES 2 ½ CUPS (600 ML)

A delicious, full-flavoured dressing for the fall.

Directions

1. Combine in food processor sherry, green onions, garlic, parmesan, egg, lemon juice and balsamic vinegar, and pulse twice.
2. Add regular mushrooms, pulse twice.
3. Slowly add olive and vegetable oils.
4. Then add shiitake mushrooms, salt and pepper.

Ingredients

1 1/2 oz dry cooking sherry (45 mL)
1/4 cup green onion (60 mL)
1 tsp minced garlic (5 mL)
1 tbsp parmesan cheese (15 mL)
1 large egg
1 oz lemon juice (30 mL)
1 oz balsamic vinegar (30 mL)
1/2 cup regular mushrooms (120 mL)
3 1/4 oz olive oil (98 mL)
6 1/2 oz vegetable oil (195 mL)
1/2 cup shiitake mushrooms,
grilled then sliced (120 mL)
2 pinches of salt
2 pinches of pepper

Sauces

Creole Sauce/34

Blackened Tomato Salsa/35

Czarina Sauce/36

Peanut Butter Dipping Sauce/37

Honey-Soya-Rosemary Sauce/38

Southwest Cilantro Sauce/39

Creole Sauce

MAKES 6 CUPS (720 ML)

We use Creole Sauce on our Jambalaya in the restaurant, but this versatile sauce can also be served with pasta, added to fish or meat, or even served at brunch with eggs. In summertime, we replace the canned tomatoes with fresh.

Ingredients

2 whole bay leaves
1 tsp oregano (5 mL)
1 tsp salt (5 mL)
1/2 tsp white pepper (2.5 mL)
1/2 tsp cayenne (2.5 mL)
1/2 tsp paprika (2.5 mL)
1/2 tsp black pepper (2.5 mL)
1/2 tsp thyme (2.5 mL)
1/2 tsp basil (2.5 mL)
1/4 cup unsalted butter (60 mL)
1/4 cup olive oil (60 mL)
1 cup onions, chopped (240 mL)
1 cup celery, chopped (240 mL)
1 cup green peppers, chopped (240 mL)
1 1/2 tsp minced garlic (7.5 mL)
1 1/4 cups chicken stock (300 mL)
3 cups canned plum tomatoes, crushed (720 mL)
1 cup canned chili sauce (240 mL)

Directions

1. Thoroughly combine bay leaves, oregano, salt, white pepper, cayenne, paprika, black pepper, thyme, and basil, and set aside.
2. Heat oil and butter in a large skillet over medium heat.
3. Stir in onions, celery and green peppers, and sauté until onions are translucent but firm, approximately 5 minutes.
4. Add garlic and seasoning mix, and cook for 5 minutes, stirring occasionally.
5. Stir in the stock, tomatoes and chili sauce, and bring to a boil.
6. Reduce heat and simmer sauce for about 20 minutes.
7. Remove bay leaves and adjust salt before serving.

Blackened Tomato Salsa

MAKES 10 OUNCES (300 ML)

Elena invented this dish when she discovered blackening tomatoes gives them a nice, smoky flavour. This favourite salsa goes well with blue corn chips, baked polenta or barbecued meats and fish.

Directions

1. Coat the pieces of tomato with blackening mix and place on a hot cast iron pan. (See Lagniappe).
2. Drizzle with melted butter to get a smoky taste, flip and repeat on other side.
3. Cut the blackened tomatoes into cubes.
4. Combine salsa ingredients and add tomatoes.

An alternative...

This sauce is a great beginning for an excellent gazpacho. To make gazpacho from this salsa combine and add the following to the above mixture. Let sit for about 1 hour. Serve chilled.

2 cups tomato juice (1/2 L)
1 cucumber, peeled, seeded and chopped
salt and pepper

Ingredients

6 tomatoes, 1/2" (2.5 cm) slices
blackening mix (see Lagniappe)

Salsa Ingredients

1/2 cup purple onions,
finely chopped (120 mL)
1/2 cup green onions,
chopped (120 mL)
1 1/2 tbsp jalapenos, chopped, with
seeds (22.5 mL)
1/2 cup chopped cilantro (120 mL)
1/2 cup olive oil (120 mL)
1 tbsp salt (15 mL)
1/2 cup lemon juice (120 mL)

Czarina Sauce

MAKES SIX TO EIGHT PORTIONS

*This can be served on bronzed salmon or chicken. If you are using this as a sauce for a pasta dish,
you can add more seafood.*

Ingredients

1/2 lb unsalted butter (227 g)

1 cup carrots, peeled and
julienned (240 mL)

1 cup purple onions, julienned (240 mL)

1 cup zucchini, peeled and
julienned (240 mL)

1 cup yams, peeled and
julienned (240 mL)

1 lb peeled crawfish tails
or shrimp (454 g)

1 tsp lemon juice (5 mL)

1 cup heavy cream (240 mL)

1/2 cup finely grated parmesan
cheese (120 mL)

Directions

1. In a large skillet on medium heat melt half the butter. Add carrots and sauté 1 minute.
2. Add onions and cook 1 minute.
3. Add zucchini and yams, and cook for about 2 to 3 minutes, until the vegetables are bright.
4. Add crawfish or shrimp, lemon juice and remaining butter, and cook until the butter is half melted.
5. Add cream and cook for about 3 minutes, until butter is completely melted and the sauce comes to a boil, stirring frequently.
6. Add the parmesan cheese and continue cooking for about 3 minutes, until the cheese has melted and the sauce has thickened a little. If oil starts to separate, add a little more cream and stir until blended.

Peanut Butter Dipping Sauce

SERVES SIX TO EIGHT

This sauce is perfect with vegetable crudité or chicken satays.

Directions

1. In a food processor, combine peanut butter, whipping cream, hot sauce, peppers and honey. Pulse until thoroughly mixed. This sauce can be kept for up to 2 weeks in a tightly sealed jar.

Ingredients

1/2 cup crunchy peanut butter (125 g)
3 1/2 oz Louisiana style hot sauce (100 mL)
5 oz whipping cream (150 mL)
1 jalapeno pepper, chopped and seeded
2 tbsp honey (30 mL)

Honey–Soya–Rosemary Sauce

Makes 2 cups (480 mL)

We created this sauce while planning our staff picnic. Elena asked Jami to create a sauce to complement our spit-roasted suckling pig. The result was nick-named "the pig dip." At the same time, we were searching for a new sauce to serve with our Black Swamp Shrimp, and decided this would be perfect! Besides shrimp, we also recommend it be served with barbecued pork chops.

Ingredients

1/4 cup soya sauce (60 mL)
1/2 cup hot sauce (120 mL)
1/4 cup Worcestershire sauce (60 mL)
1 tsp black pepper (5 mL)
2 tsp cayenne (10 mL)
1 cup honey (240 mL)
4 tbsp fresh rosemary (60 mL)
2 tbsp dried tarragon (30 mL)
1 tbsp chili flakes (15 mL)

Directions

1. In a food processor combine soya sauce, hot sauce, Worcestershire sauce, black pepper, cayenne and honey until blended.
2. Add chopped rosemary, tarragon and chili flakes, and pulse until well combined. This sauce can be kept in the refrigerator for up to 15 days.

Southwest Cilantro Sauce

MAKES 20 OUNCES (600 ML)

We have served this sauce with blackened shrimp and catfish fingers as weekly specials — everyone raved.

Directions

1. In a food processor combine and purée onions, lime juice, cilantro and hot sauce.
2. Add eggs, salt, pepper and continue to process.
3. With the machine running, slowly stream in the olive oil until completely incorporated.

Ingredients

1/4 cup green onion, chopped (60 mL)
1/2 cup lime juice (120 mL)
1 cup fresh, chopped cilantro (240 mL)
2 tbsp Louisiana-style hot sauce (30 mL)
2 eggs
salt and pepper to taste
1 1/2 cups olive oil (360 mL)

Appetizers

Crawfish Boil/42
Smoked Salmon Crostini and Roasted Garlic Aïoli with Marinated Purple Onion/43
Roasted Garlic Aïoli/44
Baked Garlic/45
Shrimp Remoulade/46
Oysters Rockefeller/47
Pontchartrain Mussels/48
Blackened Scallops with Sweet Potato Aïoli/49
Sweet Potato Aïoli/50
Crab Cakes/51
Alligator Creole/52
Kick-Ass Andouille/53
N'Awlins Jump-up Rolls with Hot Sesame Drizzle/54
Hot Sesame Drizzle/55
Chicken Liver Pâté with Pear and Currants/56
Blackened Chicken Livers/57
Grilled Wild Mushroom Cheesecake with Green Onion Coulis/58
Green Onion Coulis/59

Crawfish Boil

We have people that come to the restaurant just for this dish. There's nothing like the taste of crawfish! The best way to serve this messy dish is to provide your guests with bibs and napkins, cover a large table with a thick layer of newspaper and pile the steaming crawfish in the centre. See the Lagniappe to find out how to eat crawfish.

Ingredients

5 1/2 oz shrimp boil spice (see Lagniappe) (165 mL)
10 lb live crawfish (4.5 kg)
4 onions, unpeeled and chopped
4 celery stalks with leaves, chopped
3 lemons, sliced
1/2 bunch fresh parsley
3 whole scallions, chopped
1 head garlic, unpeeled and chopped
1/2 oz cayenne (15 mL)
1 cup red wine (240 mL)
1 tbsp salt (15 mL)
2 tbsp black pepper (30 mL)
1 lb small new red potatoes, unpeeled (454 g)
4 corn-on-the-cob, 1/2 per person

Directions

1. Fill a large pot about a third full with water and add all ingredients except crawfish, corn and potatoes.
2. Bring to a rolling boil and cook for 30 minutes on high heat to make a rich stock.
3. Soak crawfish in salted water for 15 minutes. After this initial soaking, place them in a colander under cold running water to give them a good rinse. Discard any dead ones.
4. When thoroughly soaked, cleaned and rinsed, add the live crawfish to the stock pot.
5. Add potatoes and corn, and if not covered completely, add more water.
6. Return to boil for 15 minutes.
7. Turn off heat and test the crawfish. If it is not cooked through or doesn't taste spicy, let the whole batch soak in the hot spicy liquid for a few minutes longer. Crawfish should be deep red in colour when cooked.

Smoked Salmon Crostini and Roasted Garlic Aïoli with Marinated Purple Onion

SERVES FOUR TO SIX

How can you resist! Smoked salmon never goes out of fashion and Garlic Aïoli is a delicious complement.

Directions

1. On a baking sheet, brush the toasted slices of bread with the aïoli.
2. Top each piece with a slice of smoked salmon.
3. Broil for 3 to 4 minutes.
4. Remove from oven and top with a slice of marinated purple onion.

Ingredients

4–6 oz smoked salmon (114–170 g)

1 French stick, 1/2" (1.5 cm) slices, toasted

roasted garlic aïoli (page 44)

marinated purple onion (see Lagniappe)

Roasted Garlic Aïoli

MAKES 1 ¼ CUPS (300 mL)

A delicious addition to almost any dish —
drizzle on a baked potato, salad or soup.

Ingredients

1 head of baked garlic (page 45)
1 large egg
1 cup olive oil (240 mL)
2 tbsp fresh lemon juice (30 mL)
1 tsp salt (5 mL)
1 tsp black pepper (5 mL)

Directions

1. Pinch the baked garlic to remove the cloves. In a food processor purée the garlic and the egg.
2. With the machine running, slowly stream in the oil until the mixture is thick and emulsified.
3. Add the lemon juice, salt and pepper, and blend well.

Baked Garlic

We've been serving this dish on our menu since 1985, and I don't even remember what inspired us, but it is good! Most people can eat one head of garlic. We always suggest that two people share it — for obvious reasons!

Directions

1. Cut top of the head of garlic to expose the cloves and place in shallow baking dish.
2. Sprinkle with oregano, salt and pepper, and bake covered at 350° F (180°C).
3. Check after 30 minutes. Cloves should be soft.
4. To serve, place a head of garlic on lettuce and dribble with a little of the excess oil from the baking pan. Serve this with cubes of feta and black olives, or spread the baked garlic cloves, like pâté, over toasted slices of French stick.

Ingredients

1 full head of garlic
1 tbsp olive oil (30 mL)
2 pinches oregano
1 pinch each salt and pepper

Shrimp Remoulade

SERVES FOUR TO SIX

Remoulade (pronounced rum-a-lahd) sauce is one of the glories of Creole cuisine and Shrimp Remoulade is the most popular appetizer in New Orleans' restaurants.

Ingredients

1 lb medium shrimp, heads removed (454 g)
4 cups fish stock (page 11) (1 L)
2 tbsp salt (30 mL)
1/2 tsp ground cayenne (2.5 mL)
1/2 tsp ground white pepper (2.5 mL)
1/2 tsp ground black pepper (2.5 mL)
remoulade sauce (see Lagniappe)

Directions

1. Peel and devein the shrimp.
2. Bring the stock, salt and peppers to a full boil in a medium saucepan over high heat.
3. Drop in the shrimp and stir.
4. Continue to cook over high heat for 4 to 5 minutes, stirring often until the shrimp are pink and firm.
5. Drain the shrimp and cool them quickly in the refrigerator.
6. Serve with remoulade dipping sauce.

Oysters Rockefeller

SERVES FOUR

Oysters Rockefeller have become a symbol of New Orleans cuisine – fresh oysters on well-scrubbed shells under a thick, pungent sauce of chopped greens and seasonings. The dish was invented at Antoine's restaurant in New Orleans around the turn of the century and was named Rockefeller because it was incredibly rich. Oysters on the half shell on rock salt is the classic presentation.

Directions

1. Scrub the oysters. Open them with a shucking knife over a bowl and remove the meat, being sure to reserve all the juices. Keep the shells aside.
2. Melt butter in a skillet on medium heat and cook spinach and parsley, uncovered, until soft.
3. Add bread crumbs, Worcestershire, Tabasco, anchovy paste and Pernod, mix well and cook for 2 minutes.
4. Remove this mixture and blend in a food processor until it becomes a paste.
5. In each shell, place an oyster and 1 tbsp (15 mL) of the paste.
6. Place a thick layer of rock salt in the bottom of a baking pan and lay reassembled oysters on top.
7. Sprinkle with the oyster juice and a pinch of parmesan.
8. Bake in a preheated oven at 400°F (200°C) for 15 minutes.

NOTE: Malpeque Large, Pine Island or Martha's Vineyard are the oysters we recommend for this dish.

Ingredients

24 oysters
1/4 lb butter (114 g)
1 bunch fresh spinach, stems removed
1 cup parsley, chopped (240 mL)
1 cup bread crumbs (240 mL)
2 tbsp Worcestershire sauce (30 mL)
1 tsp Tabasco (5 mL)
2 tsp anchovy, chopped (10 mL)
2 oz Pernod (60 mL)
rock salt for serving
parmesan cheese

Pontchartrain Mussels

SERVES SIX TO EIGHT

*Mussels aren't readily available in New Orleans
but this particular mango-mussel dish found it's way onto our menu.*

Ingredients

3 lb mussels (1 1/2 kg)
1 tbsp butter (15 mL)
1 tbsp ginger, peeled and chopped (15 mL)
1/2 tsp garlic, peeled and cubed (2.5 mL)
1 ripe mango, julienned
1/4 cup carrots, julienned (60 mL)
1/4 cup celery, julienned (60 mL)
1/4 cup purple onions, julienned (60 mL)
1/8 cup green onion, julienned (30 mL)
1/8 cup red pepper, julienned (30 mL)
1/2 tsp chili flakes (2.5 mL)
1/2 tsp black pepper (2.5 mL)
pinch of salt
1 cup fish stock (page 11) (240 mL)
1 cup dry white wine (240 mL)

Directions

1. Clean mussels by scrubbing in tepid water using a soft-bristled brush and set aside.
2. Melt butter in a saucepan, and sauté ginger and garlic for 3 minutes on high heat.
3. Add mango and cook for another 5 minutes.
4. Add julienned vegetables and cook for 2 minutes.
5. Add seasonings, fish stock and wine, and bring to a boil.
6. Add the mussels and cover for 5 minutes, shaking the pan constantly. When the mussels open, they're ready to serve. Do not overcook. Discard unopened shells.

Blackened Scallops with Sweet Potato Aïoli

SERVES SIX TO EIGHT

This velvety sweet sauce is perfect with the smoky, spicy, crispy scallops.
We like to undercook the scallops for a better flavour.

Directions

1. Heat a cast iron pan until white hot, about 30 minutes (no oil). See page 125 for tips on blackening.
2. Put scallops and blackening mix into a plastic bag, and shake until coated.
3. Remove scallops from bag, and place in pan to sear and blacken.
4. Drizzle in melted butter to increase blackening, and sear scallops 1 to 2 minutes per side.
5. To serve, put 1 tbsp (15 mL) of sweet potato aïoli on an 8" (20 cm) plate, place blackened scallops, pyramid style, in the centre of the plate, and serve immediately.

Ingredients

24 large Bay scallops
1 1/2 oz Blackening spice (see Lagniappe) (42 g)
1 tsp butter (5 mL)
sweet potato aïoli (page 50)

Sweet Potato Aïoli

MAKES 1 ¼ CUPS (300 ML)

A Southern, new-wave aïoli.

Ingredients

4 medium yams
1 whole egg
1 1/2 cups olive oil (360 mL)
2 tbsp lemon juice (30 mL)
salt and pepper to taste

Directions

1. Bake yams, peels on, in the oven at 375°F (190°C) for about 30 minutes, until tender.
2. Remove the yams from the oven and let cool, then peel and place them in a food processor.
3. Add the egg and lemon juice, and purée.
4. With the machine running, stream in the olive oil slowly until completely mixed.
5. Season with salt and pepper.

Crab Cakes

MAKES 15 LARGE OR 25 SMALL CAKES

Crab cakes are as N'awlins as Gumbo.
This recipe is a restaurant favourite. Serve them with Remoulade Sauce or Swamp Tartar Sauce

Directions

1. Sauté onions and garlic in butter over medium-high heat until onions are transparent.
2. Add the cayenne, thyme, Worcestershire sauce, celery and green pepper, and sauté for 10 minutes, stirring occasionally.
3. Remove from heat and mix in crab meat, green onion, cheese, bread crumbs, eggs, salt and pepper.
4. Form mixture into patties 2" (5 cm) in diameter and about 1" (2.5 cm) high and deep-fry for 3 to 5 minutes. See page 131 for tips on frying.

Ingredients

1/4 lb butter (114 g)
1 tsp minced garlic (5 mL)
1/4 cup onions, chopped (60 mL)
1 tsp cayenne (5 mL)
1/4 tsp thyme (1.3 mL)
1/2 tsp Worcestershire sauce (2.5 mL)
1/4 cup celery, chopped (60 mL)
1/4 cup green pepper, chopped (60 mL)
1 lb crab meat (454 g)
2 tbsp green onion, chopped (30 mL)
1/4 cup parmesan cheese, freshly grated (60 ml)
2 cups bread crumbs (480 mL)
3 large eggs, beaten
salt and pepper to taste
oil for frying

51

Alligator Creole

SERVES SIX TO EIGHT

Yes, alligators are edible and they're very tasty fare when Cajun and Creole cooks go to work on them with their "hocus pocus." If you're having trouble finding alligator, you can substitute swordfish or shark.

Ingredients

1 lb alligator, cubed (454 g)
1/4 cup unsalted butter (60 mL)
1 cup onion, chopped (240 mL)
1 cup celery, chopped (240 mL)
1 cup green pepper, chopped (240 mL)
1 1/2 tsp minced garlic (7.5 mL)
1/2 tsp white pepper (2.5 mL)
1/2 tsp black pepper (2.5 mL)
1/8 tsp cayenne pepper (0.5 mL)
2 bay leaves
1 tsp salt (5 mL)
1 28-oz (840-mL) can tomatoes, chopped
1 tbsp fresh coriander (15 mL)
1/2 cup Louisiana style hot sauce (120 mL)

Directions

1. Melt butter in a large skillet.
2. On high heat sauté alligator in butter for 8 to 10 minutes until lightly brown.
3. Reduce heat to medium and stir in onions, celery and peppers and sauté until tender.
4. Add garlic, peppers, bay leaves and salt, and cook for 1 minute.
5. Stir in tomatoes, coriander and hot sauce.
6. Bring to a boil.
7. Reduce heat and simmer for 30 minutes.
8. Remove bay leaves and adjust salt.
9. Serve over pasta or rice.

NOTE: Alligator looks like chicken and does not have a very strong fish taste – it's a reptile. You can't purchase alligator in a retail store, but it is available from our restaurant. The meat of farm-raised alligator can be purchased in little packets already cut and cleaned.

Kick–Ass Andouille

SERVES SIX TO EIGHT

The ancho chili reigns supreme in this dish, and coriander adds a nice touch.
Keep the beer cold and plentiful!

Directions

1. Caramelize onions in olive oil and butter on low heat for about 1 hour, until the onions are sticky and brown but not burnt.
2. Add the Andouille and cook on high heat for another 20 minutes, until the sausages are golden.
3. Add the chilis and cook for another 5 minutes. Add Creole sauce and hot sauce, and continue cooking until sauce has thickened.
4. Add coriander and continue cooking another 5 minutes.

NOTE: We serve this dish with marinated black-eyed peas, which are available canned in most supermarkets, or dried in most health food stores.

∗ Dabloons are 1½" diameter medallions that are thrown from the Mardis Gras parade floats to the crowds along the roadsides; they become much prized possessions.

Ingredients

4 cups onions, chopped (1 L)
1/4 cup olive oil (60 mL)
1/4 lb butter (114 g)
4 Andouille sausages, cut into dabloons∗
3 tbsp ancho chili pepper (45 mL)
(steamed for 5 minutes or put into a bowl submerged in hot water for 10 minutes—remove seeds to reduce heat)
4 cups Creole sauce (page 34) (1 L)
2 cups Louisiana style hot sauce (480 mL)
1 small bunch fresh coriander, chopped

N'Awlins Jump-up Rolls with Hot Sesame Drizzle

MAKES 20 LARGE ROLLS

Since the beginning of the Thai food craze, spring rolls were added to our menu. We like to keep changing the sauce, but I like the taste of our Sesame Drizzle!

Ingredients

1 pkg 8" (20 cm) spring roll wrappers
1/2 cup vegetable oil (120 mL)
1/2 cup fresh ginger,
chopped fine (120 mL)
1 cup onion, julienned (240 mL)
1 cup red pepper, julienned (240 mL)
1 cup carrot, julienned (240 mL)
1 cup celery, julienned (240 mL)
1/4 cup soya sauce (60 mL)
1/4 cup sweet Sherry (60 mL)
1 bag egg noodles
1/2 cup coriander, chopped (120 mL)

Directions

1. Heat oil in a wok on high heat for 2 minutes.
2. Add ginger and onion, and sauté for 2 minutes.
3. Add red pepper, carrot and celery, and cook for 3 minutes, then remove from heat.
4. Add soya sauce, Sherry, egg noodles and coriander, and toss together.
5. Assemble according to the instructions on the spring rolls package. We recommend the spring roll wrappers we use, which are "Spring Home T.Y.J. Spring Roll Pastry," which can be purchased at any Asian food store.
6. Heat enough oil in a deep-fryer. Fry rolls until golden brown. See Lagniappe for tips on frying.

Hot Sesame Drizzle

MAKES 1 ¼ CUPS (300 mL)

Directions

1. In a food processor, combine sherry, soya sauce, and lemon juice and mix until combined.
2. In a separate container, combine the two oils and slowly add to the processor bowl until emulsified.
3. Remove dip from food processor and add coriander, sesame seeds and chili flakes.

Ingredients

2 tbsp sweet red sherry (30 mL)

2 tbsp soya sauce (30 mL)

1 tbsp lemon juice (15 mL)

1/2 cup olive oil (120 mL)

1/4 cup sesame oil (60 mL)

1/2 bunch fresh coriander, chopped (1/2)

2 tbsp sesame seeds, roasted (30 mL)

2 tsp chili flakes (10 mL)

Chicken Liver Pâté with Pear and Currants

MAKES 1 LB (454 G) PÂTÉ

An updated version of an old favourite with a Cajun twist.
This recipe is great at parties served with a toasted French stick. This recipe was quite a hit at a recent food show.

Ingredients

1/8 cup raisins (30 mL)
1 1/4 oz port (38 mL)
4 strips bacon
1/4 cup onion, chopped (60 mL)
1 pinch fresh garlic
1 lb chicken livers (454 g)
1 pinch nutmeg
1/2 tsp cayenne (2.5 mL)
1/2 tsp pepper (2.5 mL)
1/2 tsp blackening mix
(see Lagniappe) (2.5 mL)
1 tsp salt (5 mL)
1/8 tsp cinnamon (0.5 mL)
1 bay leaf
1 1/4 oz Wild Turkey Bourbon (37.5 mL)
1/2 pear
1 tbsp lemon juice (15 mL)

Directions

1. Soak raisins in port and warm in microwave on high for 1 minute.
2. Fry bacon until crispy. Remove from pan, and place on paper towel to remove excess grease.
3. Chop the bacon, and return to the frying pan with onions. Sauté until onions are translucent, then add garlic, and sauté for 1 minute.
5. Add livers and spices, and sauté until they become a pale colour, approximately 5 minutes.
6. Add whiskey and cook for 5 minutes. In a food processor, purée this mixture with the lemon juice.
7. Remove from processor. Add pear and current, and mix thoroughly.
8. Put into glass serving container and let cool.
9. Refrigerate until needed.

Blackened Chicken Livers

SERVES SIX TO EIGHT

One day a man from the Mississippi was dining at the restaurant and asked what we did with our chicken livers besides using them in Dirty Rice. He suggested we blacken them. We took this suggestion to heart and they are now our signature dish!

Directions

1. Place spice mix in a plastic bag and toss the livers in the spices until thoroughly coated.
2. Remove from the bag, shake off the excess and place the livers on a hot barbecue.
3. Drizzle with melted butter and allow flame to subside.
4. Flip and do the same to the other side until blackened – don't cook longer than 3 minutes total. See Lagniappe for tips on blackening.
5. Serve hot with lemon beurre (see page 69).

Ingredients

3 oz blackening mix (84 g)
3 tbsp butter, melted (45 mL)
24 pieces of liver, cut in half, fat trimmed and sinew removed

Grilled Wild Mushroom Cheesecake with Green Onion Coulis

SERVES TEN TO TWELVE

The idea of a "savory cheesecake" came from Chef Emeril's restaurant in New Orleans and is a standard for our catering buffet. You can use either grilled or roasted mushrooms and any combination of wild mushrooms, such as shiitake, porcini, and oyster.

Crust Ingredients

2 1/2 cups top-salted crackers, crushed (600 mL)

2 tbsp blackening spice (see Lagniappe) (30 mL)

1/2 lb butter, melted (228 g)

1/4 cup yellow cornmeal (medium coarse) (60 mL)

Filling ingredients

4 eggs

1 1/4 lb cream cheese, room temperature (570 g)

1 tsp salt (5 mL)

2 tsp black pepper (10 mL)

1/4 cup whipping cream (35% fat) (60 mL)

1 tsp lemon juice (5 mL)

1/4 cup green onions, chopped (60 mL)

1/4 cup parsley, chopped (60 mL)

1 1/2 cups assorted wild mushrooms, coarsely chopped (360 mL)

Directions

1. Mix crackers, blackening spice, cornmeal and melted butter in a bowl, and set aside.
2. Press the mixture into a 10" (25.5 cm) spring form pan and refrigerate.
3. In a food processor purée eggs, cream cheese, salt, black pepper, lemon juice, cream, green onions and parsley until smooth.
4. Remove to a bowl and add mushrooms.
5. Pour into prepared crust and bake at 350°F (180°C) for 45 minutes until cheesecake is firm to the touch and golden brown in colour.
6. Remove from the oven and allow to cool in the pan. Once cooled, refrigerate until ready to serve.
7. It should be served at room temperature, on a bed of green onion coulis (page 59) and blackened tomato salsa.

Green Onion Coulis

MAKES 2 CUPS (480 ML)

This also makes a great dip with vegetable crudité.

Directions

1. In a food processor combine the jalapeno, green onion, parsley and lemon juice and purée.
2. Add the eggs, salt and pepper, and continue to process.
3. With the machine still running, add the olive oil in a steady, slow stream until it is completely blended.
4. Serve immediately.

Ingredients

1 jalapeno pepper
3/4 cup green onion (180 mL)
1/2 cup parsley (120 mL)
3 tbsp lemon juice (45 mL)
2 large eggs
1 tsp salt (5 mL)
1 tsp black pepper (5 mL)
1 1/2 cups olive oil (360 mL)

Entrées

Blackened Grilled Leg of Lamb with Apricot-Ginger Mint Sauce on Rosemary Flat Bread/62
Osso Bucco/64
Orange Pecan Barbecued Ribs/65
Roulades of Chicken with Andouille and Orange Sauce/66
Blackened Chicken with Lemon Beurre/68
Plantation Roasted Duck with Pistachio-Orange-Cranberry Sauce/70
Bronzed Salmon with Spicy Hollandaise Sauce/72
Cracker Catfish with Swamp Tartar Sauce/74
Sole Queen of New Orleans with Bourbon Pecan Butter and Ginger Lime Sauce/75
Cajun Jambalaya/78
Red Beans and Rice/80
Voodoo Pasta/81
Creole Lasagna/82
Grilled Eggplant Napoleon with Pecan Couscous Salad/83
Tamales Con Quesso/84

Blackened Grilled Leg of Lamb with Apricot–Ginger Mint Sauce on Rosemary Flat Bread

SERVES SIX TO EIGHT

We served this dish at the 1995 Feast of Fields Organic Extravaganza Lunch — it was a hit. Suggested listening while preparing: The funky rhythm and blues of "Eating and Sleeping," by Earl King — one of the original Kings of Creole.

Ingredients

5–6 lb leg of lamb, de-boned and butterflied
(2–2 1/2 kg)
1 oz olive oil (30 mL)
blackening spice (page 120)
1 tsp caraway seeds (5 mL)
1 tsp fennel seeds (5 mL)
1 tsp mustard seeds (5 mL)
rosemary flat bread (page 6)
apricot–ginger mint sauce

Directions

1. Brush the leg of lamb with olive oil and roll in blackening spices and seeds.
2. Set barbecue grill on high.
3. Sear each side for 5 minutes then turn to low heat and grill until done.
4. Thinly slice the cooked lamb onto the rosemary flat bread and drizzle with apricot-ginger mint sauce.

Apricot–Ginger Mint Sauce

MAKES 2 CUPS (480 mL)

*While on a flight back from Ireland, I was reading a magazine that had this combination of flavours in a recipe.
I thought it might make a great sauce, and it did!*

Directions

1. Heat olive oil, add garlic, and cook for 5 minutes on high heat.
2. Add ginger and cook for 2 minutes.
3. Add chili flakes and cook for 1 minute.
4. Add apricots and sauté for 1 minute.
5. On low heat, add honey and soya sauce, and let the mixture reduce for 15 minutes.
6. Add mint and remove from heat to cool, then serve.

Ingredients

1/4 cup olive oil (60 mL)
1 tbsp minced garlic (15 mL)
3 oz fresh ginger, chopped (90 mL)
1 tbsp chili flakes (15 mL)
1 lb apricots, pitted and quartered (454 g)
1/4 cup soya sauce (60 mL)
1/4 cup honey (60 mL)
1 bunch fresh mint, chopped fine

Osso Bucco

The ultimate comfort food. Chef Elena had to phone her mother in Argentina for this one. A swampy blend of lima beans, and the holy trinity of cajun cooking — celery, onions and green pepper — finished off with a dash of lemon zest, this lamb stew takes some time to make ready. Suggested listening while preparing: The laid back rolling rhythms of The Dirty Dozen Brass Band's "I Used to Love Her."

Lamb Ingredients

6 pieces of 1" (2.5 cm) thick lamb shank
(do not use veal)
1 cup flour (240 mL)
5 tbsp blackening mix (see Lagniappe) (75 mL)
3 tbsp olive oil, for searing (45 mL)

Bean Mixture Ingredients

1 cup red wine (240 mL)
3 cups lima beans, cooked (720 mL)
1/4 cup rosemary (60 mL)
1/4 cup lemon zest (60 mL)
6 cups Creole sauce (page 34) (1.4 L)
2 cups stock (480 mL)
salt and pepper to taste

Directions

1. Combine flour and blackening mix, and coat lamb.
2. Heat oil on high and sear the pieces in a stainless steel pan until brown and crispy. Do not let it burn.
3. Transfer meat to a large roasting pan or, preferably, a cast iron one.
4. Combine ingredients for bean mixture and mix well.
5. Top lamb with bean mixture and bake at 350°F (180°C) for about 2½ hours.
6. Sprinkle with lemon zest and serve with mashed potatoes.

Orange Pecan Barbecued Ribs

SERVES SIX

Succulent pork ribs, prepared in the preferred Southern style — barbecued! This dish is strengthened by an exotic blend of oranges and pecans. Suggested listening: The bottleneck guitar of Barbecue Bob's "Goin' Up the Country" is the ideal mate for this dish.

Directions

1. If using loin ribs, cut into 2-rib pieces. Marinate ribs overnight in beer.
2. Combine, mix and sift spice ingredients.
3. Drain ribs and place in a single layer in a roasting pan. Sprinkle evenly on both sides with spice mixture, pressing in with fingers.
4. Bake ribs in oven at 350°F (180°C), until browned. Check after 30 minutes.
5. Fry the bacon in a 2-qt (2-L) saucepan on high, until crisp.
6. Add onions, and cook for 8 to 10 minutes, until brown but not burnt.
7. Add spices and garlic, and mix well.
8. Add chili sauce, honey, pecans, orange and lemon juice, rinds and pulp, stirring well.
9. Add the stock and bring to a boil, then reduce to low heat and cook for 15 minutes.
10. Add butter and stir until melted. Remove pot from heat.
11. Pour mixture into food processor and mix 10 to 20 seconds.
12. In saucepan, add puréed sauce to ribs, turn heat to high and bring sauce to a boil, then reduce heat and simmer 10 minutes, stirring constantly.
13. Remove from heat and serve immediately.

Ingredients

1 tbsp sweet paprika (15 mL)

1 tsp each salt, onion powder, garlic powder, cayenne (5 mL)

3/4 tsp each ground black and white pepper (4 mL)

1/2 tsp each thyme and oregano (2.5 mL)

3 lb country style or baby back loin ribs (1.4 kg)

2 bottles of beer

1/4 lb bacon (114 g)

3/4 cup onion (180 mL)

1 tsp minced garlic (5 mL)

1 1/4 cup chili sauce (300 mL)

3/4 cup honey (180 mL)

3/4 cup roasted pecans, chopped (180 mL)

5 tbsp orange juice (75 mL)

1/2 orange rind & pulp

2 tbsp lemon juice (30 mL)

1/2 lemon rind & pulp

1 1/2 cups chicken stock (360 mL)

2 tbsp unsalted butter (30 mL)

Roulades of Chicken with Andouille and Orange Sauce

SERVES FOUR TO SIX

Haute cuisine with a Cajun twist. The Southern taste of Andouille with an orange sauce makes this dish especially appealing. Laissez les bon temps rouler! Suggested listening while preparing: "Let the Good Times Roll," by New Orleans' Sweethearts of The Blues, Shirley and Lee.

Ingredients

4 large, whole chicken breasts
1/4 cup butter (60 mL)
2 cups onions, chopped (480 mL)
1 tsp minced garlic (5 mL)
2 Andouille sausage, coarsely chopped
1 tsp cayenne (5 mL)
1 tsp oregano (5 mL)
1 tsp chili pepper (5 mL)
2 tsp salt (10 mL)
2 tbsp coriander (30 mL)
1 tbsp fresh basil, chopped (15 mL)
1 tbsp orange peel (15 mL)
1 cup chicken stock (240 mL)

Directions

1. Remove skin and bone and place the chicken between wax paper or plastic wrap and pound with a meat tenderizer. Be careful not to make any holes in the chicken.
2. In a frying pan on medium-high heat, melt the butter, add onions and cook until crisp and golden brown.
3. Add the garlic and cook for 3 minutes.
4. Add Andouille and cook for 2 minutes.
5. Add the seasonings and cook for 2 minutes.
6. Remove from heat and cool.
7. Place cooled mixture into a food processor and pulse 4 times. Add orange peel.
8. Place the chicken on an 11" x 17" (28 x 45 cm) piece of tin foil, with edges overlapping.
9. Place the Andouille mixture in the centre of the chicken and roll.
10. Close the tin foil ends, place in the baking pan with the chicken stock and cook in the oven at 375°F (190°C) for 45 to 50 minutes.
11. Serve sliced into 1" (2.5 cm) thick rounds, drizzled with orange sauce.

Orange Sauce

Makes 2 cups (480 mL)

An up-spiced version of the traditional sauce.

Directions

1. Heat butter in saucepan, add onion and cook until translucent.
2. Add ginger and cook for 5 minutes.
3. Add orange juice and marmalade and stir. Add cayenne and salt.
4. Bring to a boil and reduce sauce by half.
5. Add cream and orange peel and cook on low heat for another 15 minutes. Serve immediately.

Ingredients

2 tbsp butter (30 mL)
1 cup onion, chopped (240 mL)
1/2 cup fresh ginger, chopped (120 mL)
1 cup orange marmalade (240 mL)
2 cups orange juice (480 mL)
1 tsp cayenne (5 mL)
2 tsp salt (10 mL)
1 tsp chili flakes (5 mL)
1 cup whipping cream (35% fat) (240 mL)
1/2 cup orange peel (120 mL)

Blackened Chicken with Lemon Beurre

SERVES SIX TO EIGHT

Eleven different spices flavour this popular platter. Blackening, a New Orleans method of cooking, was made famous by Paul Prudhomme of Louisiana. We added the lemon beurre touch. Suggested listening: Set the scene for hot and spicy chicken with Rockin' Sidney's "Hot Stepper's Dance Zydeco."

Ingredients

3 oz blackening mix (see Lagniappe) (84 g)
3 tbsp butter, melted (45 mL)
6 chicken breasts, de-boned and skinned

Directions

1. Place blackening mix in a plastic bag and toss the chicken in the spices until thoroughly coated. Set aside.
2. Set gas grill at high heat. See Lagniappe for tips on blackening
3. Put chicken on grill and drizzle with melted butter. Allow flame to subside.
4. Flip and do the same to the other side – this will blacken the meat. If it is not cooked through, finish in the oven or on the side of the barbecue where the heat is low.
6. Serve with lemon beurre.

Lemon Beurre

A traditional French sauce.
People always ask for more — it's so good!

Directions

1. In a heavy-bottomed saucepan, combine sugar and lemon juice and bring to a boil, then immediately reduce to simmer.
2. Cook until sauce is reduced by half (should be thick enough to coat a spoon).
3. While still simmering, drop in the butter, one piece at a time, stirring constantly.
4. Once the butter has all been melted, remove from heat, stir in the cream and then cool for 1 hour. This sauce can be kept refrigerated for about 1 week.

Ingredients

1/2 cup white sugar (120 mL)
1/2 cup fresh lemon juice (120 mL)
1/4 lb butter, cut into 4 pieces (114 g)
2 cups whipping cream (35% fat) (480 mL)

Plantation Roasted Duck with Pistachio–Orange–Cranberry Sauce

SERVES FOUR TO SIX

This dish is so grand, any plantation would be honoured to serve it. Suggested listening while preparing: The Dixieland jazz sounds of the legendary Preservation Hall Jazz Band's "Lou-Easy-An-I-A."

Ingredients

1/4 cup clarified butter (60 mL)
1 tbsp blackening mix (see Lagniappe) (15 mL)
1 whole duck
2 cups orange juice (480 mL)
2 cups chicken stock (480 mL)

Stuffing Ingredients

1 oz butter (28 g)
1 1/2 cups onions, chopped (360 mL)
1 tsp garlic (5 mL)
1 tsp ginger (5 mL)
1/4 cup orange peel (60 mL)
1/4 cup coriander, chopped (60 mL)
salt and pepper
1/4 cup pistachios (60 mL)
2 cups jalapeno corn bread, crumbled
(page 3) (480 mL)

Roasting the duck...

1. Mix clarified butter and blackening mix, and rub on the duck.
2. Place stuffing into the duck cavity, and place in a roasting pan with the orange juice and chicken stock.
3. Cook for 1½ hours at 400°F (200°C).
4. Serve with pistachio-orange-cranberry sauce.

Making the stuffing

1. Heat butter in a skillet on medium-high. Add onions and sauté until brown.
2. Add garlic and ginger and cook for 3 minutes.
3. Add the orange peel and cook for 2 minutes.
4. Add the salt and pepper and cook for 2 minutes.
5. Add the coriander, pistachios and crumbled corn bread. Toss well and set aside until ready to stuff duck.

Making the sauce...

1. Heat butter in a skillet. Add onions and cook until translucent.
2. Add garlic and ginger and cook for 5 minutes.
3. Add fresh cranberries, orange marmalade and peel, and cook 15 minutes.
4. Add pistachios, sugar and chili flakes, and cook for 5 minutes.
5. Add the salt, pepper and orange juice, and reduce liquid over a low heat for about 20 minutes. Sauce should be thick.
6. Serve with Plantation Roast Duck.

Ingredients for Pistachio Orange Cranberry Sauce

1/4 cup butter (60 mL)

1 cup onions, chopped (240 mL)

1 tsp garlic, minced (5 mL)

1/4 cup fresh ginger, minced (60 mL)

2 cups fresh cranberries (480 mL)

1/2 cup orange marmalade (120 mL)

1/4 cup orange peel (60 mL)

1 cup roasted pistachios, chopped (240 mL)

salt and pepper to taste

3 cups orange juice (720 mL)

1 tbsp brown sugar (15 mL)

1 tsp chili flakes (5 mL)

Bronzed Salmon with Spicy Hollandaise Sauce

SERVES SIX

Bronzing is a lighter form of blackening using more herbs and less spice. Add some zip with a cayenne hollandaise à la The Big Easy. Suggested listening while preparing: The hard core R & B sounds of "She's Got Me, Hook, Line & Sinker," by Smiley Lewis.

Ingredients

6 salmon fillets, 4–5 oz (114–142 g) each
2 tbsp butter, melted (30 mL)
3 tbsp bronzing mix (page 120) (45 mL)

Directions

1. Rinse fillets quickly under cold running water and blot with paper towels.
2. Coat salmon with bronzing spices.
3. In a hot stainless steel pan arrange fillets in a single layer and drizzle with half of the butter. Cook about half a minute.
4. With a large spatula, turn fish and drizzle with remaining butter.
5. Cook until fish is cooked through and flakes when tested with the tip of a knife (about 5 additional minutes).
6. Serve with spicy hollandaise or czarina sauce (page 36).

NOTE: Do not use a caste-iron pan for this method.

Spicy Hollandaise Sauce

MAKES 1 ¼ CUPS (300 mL)

A kick and a twist on the traditional sauce.

Directions

1. In the top of a double-boiler, over gently simmering water, combine egg yolks, water and wine.
2. Whisk until mixture thickens and is shiny, about 2 minutes. Remove from heat once or twice during the whisking to avoid curdling.
3. Remove from heat and continue beating while slowly adding butter.
4. Beat in the Worcestershire sauce, cayenne, Tabasco sauce and lemon juice until fully mixed. The sauce should be light and fluffy.

Ingredients

2 egg yolks
3 tsp water (15 mL)
4 tsp white wine (20 mL)
4 oz clarified butter, warm (114 g)
1 tsp Worcestershire sauce (5 mL)
1/4 tsp cayenne pepper (1.25 mL)
1 tbsp Tabasco sauce (15 mL)
1 tsp lemon juice (5 mL)

Cracker Catfish with Swamp Tartar Sauce

How can a fish with such an ugly face taste so good? Now farm-raised everywhere! Jazz it up with a side of tartar sauce with a French Quarter spin. Suggested listening while preparing: Louis Armstrong's jazzy take on the classic "Do You Know What It Means To Miss New Orleans."

Ingredients

6-8 catfish fillets, 6-7 oz
(170-200 g) each
olive oil
3 cups salted crackers, crumbled (720 mL)
1 cup cornmeal (240 mL)
1 cup flour (240 mL)
1 cup blackening mix (see Lagniappe)

Swamp Tartar Ingredients

1/2 cup green onions (120 mL)
1/2 cup parsley, chopped (120 mL)
2 tbsp mustard (30 mL)
1/4 cup white vinegar (60 mL)
1/4 cup jalapeno peppers, chopped (60 mL)
1 cup cornichons (240 ml)
1 cup mayonnaise (240 mL)
1/4 cup capers, chopped (60 mL)

Directions

1. Dip fillets in olive oil.
2. Combine crackers, cornmeal, flour and blackening mix, and completely coat oil-coated fillets.
3. Bake in oven at 375°F (190°C) for 30 minutes. If the surface of the fish bounces back when poked, it's done.

Making the sauce...

1. In a food processor combine green onions, parsley, mustard, vinegar, jalapenos and cornichons. Pulse 3 times.
2. Remove sauce to a bowl, mix with mayonnaise and capers and serve.

Sole Queen of New Orleans with Bourbon Pecan Butter and Ginger Lime Sauce

SERVES SIX

Sole, the delicate white-fleshed fish is the queen of the water in the Gulf of Mexico. A traditional dish in "The City that Care Forgot," this sea fare is well chaperoned by bourbon and pecans. Suggested listening while preparing: Irma Thomas, the Sole Queen of New Orleans doing her famous "Second Line Medley: I Done Got Over/Iko/Iko/Hey Pocky Way."

Directions

1. Wash the greens well and steam.
2. Pat the fillets dry and place one fillet on the centre of each leaf.
3. Add a dollop of bourbon pecan butter to the centre of each fillet.
4. Fold each of the four sides of the leaf to cover the fish.
5. Place each leaf-wrapped fillet into a baking dish with the fish stock, and cook for 20 minutes at 375°F (190°C).
6. Serve with ginger lime sauce (page 77).

Ingredients

6 leaves of collard greens
6 fillets of sole, 6 oz (170 g) each
1 cup fish stock (page 11) (240 mL)
bourbon–pecan butter (page 76)

75

Bourbon–Pecan Butter

Ingredients

1/2 lb butter, unsalted (228 g)
1 cup pecans (240 mL)
1 cup bourbon (240 mL)
1 tsp salt (5 mL)
1/2 tsp black pepper (2.5 mL)
1/2 tsp blackening mix
(see Lagniappe) (2.5 mL)

Directions

1. Combine and mix all ingredients in a food processor.
2. Shape the mixture into a log, roll the butter in plastic wrap and store in the fridge for at least 1 hour before using.
3. Slice into disks when using.

76

Ginger Lime Sauce

MAKES 2 CUPS (480 mL)

Directions

1. Heat butter in a saucepan and cook onions until crispy and golden brown.
2. Add garlic, ginger, chili peppers and salt, and cook for 3 to 5 minutes.
3. Add lime zest and cook for 2 minutes.
4. Add lime juice and cook for another 5 minutes.
5. Add candied ginger syrup. Stir well and then add cream.
6. Bring to a boil and cook sauce until thickened.

Ingredients

1/4 lb butter (114 g)

1 cup onions, chopped (240 mL)

1/8 tsp garlic (0.5 mL)

1/2 cup fresh ginger, minced (120 mL)

1/8 tsp chili peppers (0.5 mL)

2 tsp salt (10 mL)

1/2 cup lime zest (120 mL)

1/4 cup lime juice (60 mL)

1/2 cup candied ginger syrup (120 mL)

1/2 cup whipping cream (35% fat) (120 mL)

Cajun Jambalaya

The time-honoured Cajun combination of baked rice, poultry, shrimp, Andouille sausage and cayenne, was embraced by the Crescent City. They added tomatoes to make it their own. This Southern Accent favourite deserves an upbeat jump-up musical accompaniment. Suggested listening while preparing: If you're cooking Cajun style, Jo El Sonnier's zydeco version of "Jambalaya" is required. If you're adding tomatoes to the mix, check out "Dans Le Jumbo" by Compagnie Creole.

Spice Ingredients

1 tsp cayenne (5 mL)
3/4 tsp white pepper (3.7 mL)
3/4 tsp black pepper (3.7 mL)
1 tsp cumin (5 mL)
1 tsp dried thyme (5 mL)
1 tsp dried basil (5 mL)
2 bay leaves
1 1/2 tsp salt (7.5 mL)

Directions

1. In a large kettle or Dutch oven combine butter, vegetable oil and olive oil, and heat to sizzle, then add onions.
2. On low heat cook onions for 1 to 2 hours, stirring frequently, until onions are caramelized and quite dark but not burnt – this gives the jambalaya it's distinctive colour and nutty flavour.
3. Add sliced mushrooms and sauté until soft, about 4 minutes.
4. Add celery and green peppers, and sauté for 8 minutes.
5. Add garlic and chicken, and sauté until beef colours slightly.

Continued…

6. Add ham and sausage, and cook for 5 minutes.
7. Add combined spices, stir thoroughly and cook 2 minutes.
8. Add preheated stock and bring to a boil, scraping pan bottom.
9. Add rice and shrimp and return to boil. Cover pot and bake at 350°F (180°C) for 40 to 45 minutes.
10. Remove from oven, stir thoroughly, cover and let stand 15 minutes before serving.

Jambalaya Ingredients

1/4 cup butter (60 mL)
1/4 cup vegetable oil (60 mL)
1/4 cup olive oil (60 mL)
4 cups onion, chopped (960 mL)
2 cups mushrooms, sliced (480 mL)
1 1/2 cups celery, chopped (360 mL)
1 1/2 cups green pepper, chopped (360 mL)
1 tbsp garlic, minced (15 mL)
1/2 lb chicken, cubed (228 g)
1/2 lb Andouille, sliced
and roasted (228 g)
1/2 lb ham, cubed (228 g)
1/2 lb baby shrimp, uncooked (228 g)
5 cups hot chicken stock (1.2 L)
2 1/4 cups white rice, uncooked (530 mL)

Red Beans and Rice

SERVES SIX TO EIGHT

Cajuns in Louisiana traditionally served this on Mondays — while the pot was cooking and the laundry was being done. In New Orleans' restaurants, this dish has become the one to serve on Mondays, following festive weekends of rich food and drinking. Emeril's restaurant has a red been soup on Tuesdays (they're closed Mondays) for those who missed their Monday routine. Suggested listening while preparing: The barrelhouse piano style of Professor Longhair's "Red Beans".

Ingredients

2 lb dried red kidney beans (1 kg)
2 cups onion, chopped (240 mL)
1/2 cup green onion, thinly sliced (120 mL)
1/2 cup green pepper, chopped (120 mL)
1 1/3 tbsp garlic, finely minced (20 mL)
2 tbsp parsley, finely minced (30 mL)
1 lb baked ham, cubed (454 g)
1 lb ham hock (non-smoked) (454 g)
1 tbsp salt (15 mL)
1/2 tsp freshly ground black pepper (2.5 mL)
1/8 tsp cayenne (0.5 mL)
1/8 tsp crushed chili flakes (0.5 mL)
2 whole bay leaves, in quarters
1/2 tsp dried thyme (2.5 mL)
1/8 tsp dried basil (0.5 mL)
8 cups cold water (2 L)
3 cups boiled rice (720 mL)

Directions

1. Soak beans overnight in cold water to cover. Drain in a colander and combine with all the other ingredients in a heavy 8- to 10-quart (2- to 4-Litre) pot or kettle. Add just enough water to cover.
2. Bring to a boil over high heat, then lower heat and simmer for 2½ to 3 hours, until beans are tender and a thick natural gravy has formed.
3. Toward the end of cooking, add 1 cup (240 mL) of water if the mixture appears too dry.
4. During cooking, stir frequently and scrape down the sides and across the bottom of the pot with a wooden spoon or spatula to prevent scorching.
5. Stir the entire mixture thoroughly just once every half hour.
6. When beans are cooked, turn off heat and remove ham hock. Remove skin from ham hock. Cut meat into chunks and return to mixture.
8. To serve, mound the rice in the centre of a heated plate and spoon a generous amount of bean mixture on top.

Voodoo Pasta

SERVES FOUR TO SIX

A mystical spicy Crescent City cream sauce, tossed with seafood and pasta, this dish is a melange of the powerful flavours of the South. Suggested listening while preparing: The bewilderingly pulsating beat of "Zu Zu Man" by New Orleans' Night Tripper, Dr. John.

Directions

1. Boil water and cook pasta until al dente.
2. On medium, heat cream and seafood stock in a saucepan.
3. Combine ingredients for Voodoo paste.
4. As liquid is heating, add Voodoo paste and blend well with a spatula.
5. Cook a few minutes to slightly reduce liquid.
6. Add seafood and cook until done. (This only takes a short time, approximately 2 minutes).
7. If the sauce becomes too thick, it can be thinned with a little extra stock. Be careful not to dilute the sauce.
8. Pour mixture over pasta and serve immediately.

NOTE: Use any combination of fish and shellfish as long as it is solid enough to hold together during cooking. Voodoo paste can be stored in the refrigerator for up to 2 months.

Ingredients

2 cups fish stock (page 11) (1/2 L)
1 1/2 lb multicoloured fusilli (680 g)
3 cups whipping cream (35% fat) (3/4 L)
4 tsp Voodoo paste (20 mL)
1 lb shrimp (454 g)
1/2 lb scallops (227 g)
1/2 lb squid, cleaned and cut into rings (227 g)
green onions to garnish

Voodoo Paste

4 tbsp each cayenne and paprika (60 mL)
6 tbsp salt (90 mL)
2 tbsp gumbo file (30 mL)
6 tbsp garlic (90 mL)
2 tbsp thyme (30 mL)
1/2 cup olive oil (120 mL)
1 8-oz (240 mL) can V-8 juice

Creole Lasagna

SERVES SIX TO EIGHT

The collard greens add a nice touch to this dish. Monterey Jack spices up the cheeses and Creole sauce adds that special flavour. We serve this with a simple green salad and crusty Italian bread. Suggested listening while preparing: The old-time jazz sounds of "That's A Plenty," by Kid Ory's Creole Jazz Band.

Ingredients

1/2 cup olive oil (120 mL)

2 cups onion, chopped (480 mL)

1 tsp minced garlic (5 mL)

1 large eggplant, cubed

1/4 cup parsley, chopped (60 mL)

1/4 cup coriander, chopped (60 mL)

1 cup roasted red pepper, chopped (240 mL)

1/2 tsp salt (2.5 mL)

1/2 tsp black pepper (2.5 mL)

1/2 tsp blackening mix
(see Lagniappe) (2.5 mL)

1 package lasagna noodles (prepared according to package instructions)

1/2 cup goat cheese, cubed (120 mL)

1/2 cup Monterey Jack cheese, cubed (120 mL)

1/2 cup mozzarella cheese, cubed (120 mL)

1/2 cup cheddar cheese, cubed (120 mL)

1 bunch collard greens, washed

3 cups Creole sauce (page 34) (720 mL)

1/4 cup parmesan cheese (120 mL)

Directions

1. On medium-high, heat oil in skillet, add onions and cook till crispy and golden brown.
2. Add garlic and cook for 3 minutes.
3. Add eggplant and cook for 8 minutes. Then add parsley, coriander and red pepper, and mix well.
4. Add salt, pepper and blackening mix.
5. Combine and set aside the goat, Monterey Jack, mozzarella and cheddar cheeses.
6. Pour one cup of Creole sauce in bottom of a baking dish, then place a layer of the prepared lasagna, then a layer of the collard greens, and a layer of the combined cheese mixture. Collard greens can be replaced with spinach, kale or Swiss chard.
7. Continue this until the ingredients are used up then top with 2 cups of the Creole sauce and sprinkle with parmesan.
8. Bake at 350°F (180°C) for 30 to 40 minutes. Serve hot with remaining Creole sauce.

Grilled Eggplant Napoleon with Pecan Couscous Salad

SERVES SIX TO EIGHT

This dish looks exotic and tastes marvelous. People who don't like eggplant have been converted. Suggested listening while preparing: Try the jazz sounds of Duke Robillard & His Pleasure Kings', "Too Hot to Handle."

Directions

1. Rub eggplant slices with olive oil and coat with blackening mix.
2. Grill the slices over medium heat, and set aside.
3. In a baking dish layer the eggplant, tomato and cheese slices, so that the top layer is eggplant.
4. Bake for 20 minutes at 350°F (180°C).
5. Follow directions on package to prepare couscous.
6. Add remaining salad ingredients to couscous and toss well.
7. Serve grilled eggplant napoleon over pecan couscous salad with Creole sauce (page 34).

Ingredients

6 medium eggplants, cut into 1/2" (1.3 cm) slices

1/4 cup olive oil (60 mL)

1 tsp blackening mix (see Lagniappe) (5 mL)

Fried green tomato slices (page 92)

1/2 lb Monterey Jack cheese, 1/4" (0.6 cm) slices (228 g)

Pecan Couscous Salad

1 package of couscous

1/2 cup roasted pecans (120 mL)

1/4 cup red pepper, chopped (60 mL)

1/4 cup green onions, chopped (60 mL)

1/4 cup olive oil (60 mL)

2 tbsp lemon juice (30 mL)

2 tbsp coriander, chopped (30 mL)

salt and pepper to taste

Tamales Con Quesso

SERVES SIX TO EIGHT

This has become a big favourite among our growing legion of vegetarians. Use blue cornmeal for a 'new wave' edge!
Suggested listening while preparing: "Birth of the Blues," by renowned Crescent City trumpet player Al Hirt.

Polenta Ingredients

6 tbsp olive oil (90 mL)
1/2 cup onions, chopped (120 mL)
1 tbsp minced garlic (15 mL)
2 tbsp fresh basil, chopped (30 mL)
1 tsp salt (5 mL)
2 tsp black pepper (10 mL)
1 tsp chili flakes (5 mL)
1 cup corn kernels (240 mL)
6 cups milk (1 1/2 L)
1/2 cup cheddar cheese (120 mL)
1/2 cup parmesan (120 mL)
3 tbsp parmesan, for dusting (45 mL)
3 cups organic blue cornmeal (720 mL)

Directions

1. Grease a 9" (23 cm) pan with 1 tbsp (15 mL) olive oil and set aside.
2. Heat the remaining oil, and sauté the onions and garlic until translucent.
3. Add basil, salt, pepper and chili flakes and cook further.
4. Add the corn kernels and milk and bring to a boil.
5. Slowly add the cheeses and melt completely.
6. Add the cornmeal a little at a time until the mixture has the consistency of a thick paste.
7. Remove from the heat, and working quickly, spoon half the mixture into the greased pan, spreading and packing it down.
8. Prepare filling and spread in the same manner. Add the crumbled cheeses, then top with the remaining polenta.
9. Dust with parmesan cheese and bake for 20 minutes at 375°F (190°C).

Continued…

Making the filling...

1. In a frying pan heat the butter.
2. Add the onions and cook until crispy and brown.
3. Add the garlic and cook for 3 minutes.
4. Add mushrooms and sun-dried tomatoes.
5. Remove from heat and add coriander, salt and pepper.
6. Crumble cheeses and set aside until ready to layer polenta.

Filling Ingredients

1/8 lb butter (57 g)

2 cups onions, chopped (480 mL)

1 tbsp minced garlic (15 mL)

2 cups wild mushrooms, sliced (480 mL)

1/2 cup sun-dried tomatoes, chopped (120 mL)

1/2 bunch coriander

1 cup goat cheese (240 mL)

1 cup cheddar cheese (240 mL)

salt and pepper to taste

Vegetables and Side Dishes

Southern Accent Rice/88
Dirty Rice/89
Brabant Potatoes/90
Candied Yams/90
Roasted Garlic Mashed Potatoes/91
Creole Okra/91
Corn Flap Jacks/92
Fried Green Tomatoes/92

Southern Accent Rice

SERVES SIX TO EIGHT

"Everybody can cook rice, but how come it doesn't taste like this?" Here's the answer.

Ingredients

2 cups uncooked rice (480 mL)
3 cups water (720 mL)
1 1/2 tbsp onion, chopped (23 mL)
1/2 tsp salt (2.5 mL)
1/2 tsp minced garlic (2.5 mL)
1 1/2 tbsp unsalted butter, melted (23 mL)
1/2 tsp black pepper (2.5 mL)
1/2 tsp white pepper (2.5 mL)

Directions

1. In a 9" (23 cm) loaf pan, combine all ingredients and mix well.
2. Seal the pan with aluminum foil and bake at 350°F (180°C) for 1½ hours. Serve immediately. See, it's that easy.

Dirty Rice

SERVES SIX TO EIGHT

Dirty rice is a popular Cajun dish made with chicken livers and gizzards, vegetables, rice and lots of pepper. Call it as you see it — it looks dirty. It's best to eat it on the day you cook it. You can omit the livers for a delicious rice stuffing.

Directions

1. In a large skillet heat vegetable oil on high and sauté the gizzards, pork and bay leaves until the meat is thoroughly browned (about 6 minutes), stirring occasionally.
2. Stir in the seasoning mix, then add the onion, celery, green pepper and garlic.
3. Stir thoroughly, scraping the bottom of the pan well.
4. Add butter and stir until melted.
5. Reduce heat to medium and cook for 8 minutes, stirring constantly and scraping the bottom of the pan well (to avoid excess sticking use a heavy-bottomed skillet).
6. Add the chicken stock and stir until any of the mixture sticking to the bottom of the pan comes free.
7. Cook another 8 minutes over high heat, stirring only once.
8. Stir in the chicken livers and cook for 2 minutes.
9. Add uncooked rice, stir well, cover the pan, reduce the heat to low and cook for 5 minutes.
10. Remove the skillet from heat and leave covered until the rice is tender, about 10 minutes.
11. Remove bay leaves and serve immediately.

Ingredients

2 tsp cayenne pepper (10 mL)

1 1/2 tsp each salt and black pepper, dry mustard, ground cumin (7.5 mL)

1 1/4 tsp sweet paprika (6 mL)

1/2 tsp each dried thyme and dried oregano (2.5 mL)

2 tbsp vegetable oil (30 mL)

1/2 lb chicken gizzards, ground in food processor (228 g)

1/4 lb ground pork (114 g)

2 bay leaves

1/2 cup each onion, celery, green pepper, finely chopped (120 mL)

2 tsp garlic, minced (10 mL)

3 tbsp unsalted butter (45 mL)

3 1/2 cups chicken stock (840 mL)

1/3 lb chicken livers, ground in food processor (151 g)

1 3/4 cup par boiled white rice, preferably converted (420 mL)

Brabant Potatoes

SERVES FOUR TO SIX

If you like spicy potatoes, this one's for you!

Ingredients

6 to 8 new red potatoes, boiled
and cubed

4 tbsp clarified butter (60 mL)

3 tbsp blackening mix
(see Lagniappe) (45 mL)

Directions

1. Add the clarified butter to a baking dish, add the blackening mix and combine.
2. Add the potatoes and toss well.
3. Cook in the oven for 45 minutes at 375°F (190°C) shaking the pan often so that the potatoes don't stick but will still get crispy.
4. Serve immediately

Candied Yams

SERVES FOUR TO SIX

This sweet, traditional New Orleans vegetable is a perfect accompaniment to any spicy Southern meal.

Ingredients

6 medium yams

3 tbsp vegetable oil (45 mL)

1/4 lb butter (114 g)

1 tsp nutmeg (5 mL)

3 tsp brown sugar (15 mL)

Directions

1. Peel and cut yams into small pieces.
2. Coat with oil and bake at 350°F (180°C) for 1 hour.
3. Add butter, nutmeg and sugar, and mix well.
4. Serve immediately.

Roasted Garlic Mashed Potatoes

SERVES SIX TO EIGHT

When we started serving these potatoes with the lamb on our menu, everybody wanted to order it as a side dish which drove the kitchen nuts.

Directions

1. Place potatoes in a pot of cold water, bring to a boil and cook until fork-tender.
2. Drain water, and dry potatoes in pot on low heat for 1 minute, then remove and set aside.
3. Take baked garlic, squeeze till all buds are out of husks and mash into a paste.
4. Heat up cream and butter and add to potatoes with garlic paste and mash by hand with a potato masher.
5. Add parmesan, salt and pepper

Ingredients

6 to 8 Yukon Gold potatoes
1/2 cup whipping cream (120 mL)
1/4 stick of butter (114 g)
1 head of baked garlic
1/8 cup parmesan cheese (30 mL)
salt and paper to taste

NOTE: We use Yukon Gold potatoes because they are less moist, less starchy, and have a creamy consistency.

Creole Okra

SERVES FOUR TO SIX

Team up okra with this sauce and it'll become your favourite vegetable.

Directions

1. Place okra in a baking dish with a little butter and cook at 375°F (190°C) for half an hour, then remove.
2. Heat the oil in a saucepan. Add the onions and garlic, and cook for 5 minutes.
3. Add the okra and sauté until it changes colour. Be careful not to overcook the okra – it's texture becomes too slimy.
4. Add the Creole sauce. Serve hot.

Ingredients

1 1/2 lb okra (680 g)
2 tbsp unsalted butter (30 mL)
3 tbsp olive oil (45 mL)
1 cup onions (240 mL)
1 tsp garlic (5 mL)
1 tsp black pepper (5 mL)
4 cups Creole sauce (page 34) (1 L)

Corn Flap Jacks

Serves eight

Flap Jacks can be served instead of potatoes or rice with your main course.

Ingredients

3 tbsp butter (45 mL)
1 cup corn (240 mL)
2 eggs
2 pinches of salt
1/2 tsp each baking powder, blackening spice (see Lagniappe), cumin, turmeric, chili powder, black pepper (2.5 mL)
1/2 cup each corn flour, milk (120 mL)
1/4 cup flour (60 mL)

Directions

1. Mix milk and eggs in one bowl and flours and spices in another.
2. Add egg mixture to dry mixture until completely combined.
3. On medium heat, melt butter in saucepan or heavy skillet.
4. Scoop in a spoonful of the batter, cook on one side then flip.
5. Keep warm in oven on a low heat until you've made all the corn flap jacks.

Fried Green Tomatoes

Serves six to eight

More than just a movie – a delicious side dish too!

Ingredients

1 egg
1 cup milk (240 mL)
6 beef-steak green tomatoes
1 1/2 cup cornmeal (360 mL)
1 tbsp blackening mix (see Lagniappe) (15 mL)
oil for frying

Directions

1. Beat eggs and milk in a bowl and set aside.
2. Mix cornmeal and blackening mix in a separate bowl.
3. Cut tomatoes into ½" (1 cm) slices.
4. Drown tomatoes in egg wash.
5. Drip off excess liquid and coat tomato slices with cornmeal mixture.
6. Fry for two minutes on each side until crispy and golden brown. Keep in warming oven until ready to serve.

Desserts

Basic Pastry Recipe

I like to make a whole batch of pastry dough and keep it in the freezer so it's always on hand.

Ingredients

5 cups flour (2 kg)
1 tsp salt (5 mL)
1 whole egg, beaten
3/4 cup ice-cold water (180 mL)
1/2 lb Tenderflake or vegetable
shortening (228 g)

Directions

1. Sift together flour and salt.
2. Cut Tenderflake into cubes and cut into flour/salt mixture until the mixture resembles coarse bread crumbs.
3. Combine egg and water in a separate bowl. Then slowly add the wet mixture into the dry until combined. Don't overwork the dough.
4. Divide into five portions and freeze the ones you're not using.

Beignets

MAKES 24

In New Orleans, Café du Monde is famous for these delicious doughnuts which can be served for breakfast or as a dessert.

Directions

1. Combine flour, sugar and salt, and mix well.
2. Fold in dissolved yeast, milk, eggs and butter, and continue to blend until smooth dough is formed.
3. Place dough in metal bowl, cover and allow to rise for 1 hour.
4. Remove to well-floured surface and roll out to ¼" (0.5 cm) thickness.
5. Cut into 2" x 3" (5 cm x 8 cm) rectangles and return to floured surface
6. Cover with towel again, and allow to rise.
7. Heat oil in deep-fryer to 350°F (180°C).
8. Deep fry, turning once, until golden brown.
9. Drain and dust generously with powdered sugar. Serve immediately.

Ingredients

peanut oil for frying
3 1/3 cups flour (800 mL)
1/2 cup sugar (120 mL)
1 tsp salt (5 mL)
1 pkg dry yeast, dissolved
1 1/4 cups milk (300 mL)
3 eggs, beaten
1/4 cup butter, melted (60 mL)
1 cup powdered sugar for dusting (240 mL)

Bread Pudding with Wild Turkey Bourbon Sauce

SERVES EIGHT TO TEN

*A traditional N'Awlins after-dinner treat, the addition of our Wild Turkey Bourbon Sauce turns
this one into a real "breadwinner."*

Ingredients

3 cups milk (720 mL)

3 eggs

1 cup sugar (240 mL)

1 tsp vanilla (5 mL)

3/4 tsp cinnamon (3.8 mL)

3/4 tsp nutmeg (3.8 mL)

1/4 cup unsalted butter, melted (60 mL)

1/2 cup raisins (120 mL)

1/2 cup pecans, broken (120 mL)

1 apple, diced

2 tbsp orange peel (30 mL)

4 cups dry bread, cubed, toasted (900 g)

Directions

1. Heat milk until almost boiling and remove from heat.
2. Separate eggs, and reserve egg whites.
3. With an electric mixer, beat egg yolks at high speed for 2 minutes. Add sugar a little at a time and beat well.
4. Add vanilla, nutmeg and cinnamon, and mix well.
5. Add melted butter and mix well.
6. Add hot milk mixture, raisins, pecans, apples, and orange peel, and mix well with a wooden spoon.
7. Pour mixture over bread and let soak for 1 hour.
8. Turn mixture to make sure bread is well coated.
9. Beat egg white until stiff and turn into bread mixture.
10. Fill ramekins with pudding and place in a roasting pan with 1" (2.5 cm) of water. Bake for 35 minutes at 375°F (190°C) for 10 minutes and then at 425°F (218°C), to brown.
11. Serve with Wild Turkey bourbon sauce.

Wild Turkey Bourbon Sauce

MAKES 2 CUPS (480 ML)

Directions

1. Beat eggs well with whisk, add powdered sugar, and continue beating until well mixed.
2. Melt butter in a double boiler, add egg mixture, and cook while whisking for 4 minutes.
3. Remove from heat, allow to cool. Whisk in bourbon before serving.

Ingredients

2 eggs
2 cups powdered sugar (480 mL)
1/4 lb unsalted butter (114 g)
1/4 cup Wild Turkey bourbon (60 mL)

Chocolate Banana Bread Pudding with Mint Anglaise

SERVES SIX

The proof is in the pudding. We added a new twist — bananas, chocolate and mint sauce — to an old favourite.

Ingredients

3 eggs, separated
1 ripe banana, mashed
1 French stick, cut into 1" (2.5 cm) cubes
1/2 cup pecans (120 mL)
2 1/2 cups whipping cream
(or whole milk) (600 mL)
1 tsp cinnamon (5 mL)
1 tsp vanilla (5 mL)
1/4 cup brown sugar (60 mL)
1/2 cup semisweet chocolate,
chopped (120 mL)

Directions

1. Preheat oven to 350°F (180°C).
2. Beat egg yolks until frothy and add to the mashed bananas.
3. Combine all other ingredients except egg whites and chocolate.
4. Soak the bread in the egg mixture for 1 hour.
5. Beat the egg whites until light and fluffy, and soft peaks form.
6. Fold the chocolate into the bread mixture, then fold in the egg whites, until well combined. Pour pudding mixture into ramekins or a baking dish. Place dish into a roasting pan with ½" (2.5 cm) of water and bake for 1½ hours.
7. Remove from oven and allow to cool until lukewarm.
8. To serve, spread about 2 tbsp (30 mL) of mint anglaise on each plate and top with a square of the pudding and a dollop of whipped cream. Dust with confectioners' sugar.

Mint Anglaise

MAKES 1 CUP (240 mL)

Directions

1. Combine first five ingredients, bring to a boil in a double boiler, and remove from heat.
2. Temper yolks by adding a little of the heated mixture to the yolks, thereby bringing the temperature of the yolks close to that of the heated mixture. Then slowly add the yolks to the other ingredients.
3. Return sauce to heat for 3 to 5 minutes, stirring constantly.
4. Serve with chocolate banana bread pudding.

Ingredients

1/2 cup whipping cream (35% fat) (120 mL)
1/2 tbsp mint, finally chopped (7.5 mL)
1/4 tsp crème de menthe (1.25 mL)
1 tbsp confectioners' sugar (15 mL)
1 dash vanilla
3 egg yolks

99

Butter Pecan Pie

SERVES TEN

A Southern favourite, our Butter Pecan Pie is guaranteed to melt in your mouth.

Ingredients

1 9" (23 cm) pie shell, unbaked (page 94)
3 eggs
1 tsp lemon juice (5 mL)
1 tsp vanilla (5 mL)
pinch of salt
2 tbsp butter (30 mL)
1 cup brown sugar (240 mL)
1 cup corn syrup (240 mL)
1 1/2–2 cups pecans (360–480 mL)

Directions

1. Beat eggs with a whisk until frothy. Add lemon, vanilla and salt, and mix well.
2. Melt butter and add to above.
3. Slowly add brown sugar a little at a time, beating mixture well.
4. Add corn syrup and blend well.
5. Place pecans in pie shell.
6. Cover pecans with mixture and press down pecans with hands so they get completely covered, because pecans will float to the top.
7. Bake in preheated oven at 350°F (180°C) for 40 minutes.
8. Reduce heat to 325°F (160°C) and cook for another 15 minutes or until top of pie is browned and feels firm but not dry to touch.

Butterscotch–Chocolate Pie

When serving this delicious pie you can never have too much on your plate.

Directions

1. Line 9" (23 cm) glass pie plate with crust, line with aluminum foil and weigh down with dried beans as weights. Bake at 400°F (200°C) for 10 minutes. Once crust is browned remove from oven to rack and let cool completely.
2. Reduce oven temperature to 350°F (180°C). Melt chocolate in double boiler and let cool.
4. In mixer, beat brown sugar and butter.
5. Mix in eggs, one at a time.
6. Stir in the half cup (120 mL) of cream and the melted chocolate.
7. Pour filling into prepared pie crust and bake for about 45 minutes, until the filling is set.
8. Cool pie completely.
9. Beat whipped cream and powdered sugar till stiff peaks form, and spread on pie.
10. Sprinkle with grated chocolate and serve.

Ingredients

1 9" (23 cm) pie shell (page 94)
2 oz chocolate, chopped (56 g)
2 cups brown sugar (480 mL)
1/2 cup butter (120 mL)
3 eggs
1/2 cup whipping cream (35% fat) (120 mL)

Topping

1 cup whipping cream, chilled (240 mL)
1 tbsp powdered sugar (15 mL)
1 oz grated chocolate for garnish (28 g)

Sweet Potato Pecan Pie with Praline Sauce

SERVES TEN

Give a thumbs up to our combination of two Southern staples: sweet potatoes and pecans baked in a pie.

Ingredients

pastry for 1 pie shell (page 94)
add 1/2 tsp each nutmeg, cloves
and cinnamon to the above recipe (2.5 mL)
1 cup ground pecans (240 mL)
1 tbsp butter, melted (15 mL)
1 tbsp light corn syrup (15 mL)
2 cups sweet potatoes, mashed (480 mL)
1/2 cup heavy cream (120 mL)
1/4 cup melted butter (60 mL)
2 tbsp brandy (30 mL)
1 1/2 tsp cinnamon (7.5 mL)
1 1/4 tsp nutmeg (6.25 mL)
1/2 tsp allspice (2.5 mL)
1 tsp vanilla (5 mL)
2 large eggs

Directions

1. Add spices to pastry recipe and roll out to line 10" (25 cm) tart pan.
2. Toss pecans with 1 tbsp (15 mL) butter and corn syrup, and place in pastry shell.
3. Combine other ingredients, and mix well.
4. Pour filling over nuts, and bake at 375°F (190°C) for 60 minutes.
5. If you wish, decorate the top of the pie with pecan halves before baking.
6. Serve with praline sauce or whipped cream.

Praline Sauce

MAKES 1 ½ CUPS (360 ML)

Directions

1. Combine butter and corn syrup, and boil on high heat for 10 to 15 minutes.
2. Add icing sugar, and heat until sugar is completely melted. Remove pot from heat.
3. Whisk in amaretto and chopped pecans, and let sauce cool.
4. Sauce will thicken as it cools and can be stored, covered, at room temperature until ready to serve.

Ingredients

1/4 cup butter, whipped (60 mL)
2 tbsp corn syrup (30 mL)
1/2 cup icing sugar (120 mL)
1/4 cup amaretto (60 mL)
1/2 cup roasted pecans, chopped (120 mL)

Calvados Pecan Apple Crisp

SERVES SIX

Apples marinated in brandy turns this dessert into the flavour of this or any month.

Ingredients

6 apples, cored and sliced
1/4 oz Calvados (7.5 mL)
1 pinch nutmeg
1 pinch cinnamon
1/4 cup sugar (60 mL)
dash of aromas
1 tbsp gelatin (15 mL)
1 tbsp lemon juice (15 mL)

Crumble Ingredients

1 cup brown sugar (240 mL)
1 cup all-purpose flour (240 mL)
1 cup rolled oats (240 mL)
1/2 lb butter, cold and chopped (120 mL)
1 cup almond cookies, crumbled (240 mL)
1/2 cup pecans, roughly chopped (120 mL)

Directions

1. Marinate apple slices in Calvados for 1 hour.
2. Combine sugar, nutmeg, cinnamon, gelatin, aromas and lemon juice and add to marinated apples.
3. Combine flour, sugar and oats, mixing well.
4. Cut in butter until the mixture resembles chunky bread crumbs.
5. Add cookies and pecans, and mix.
6. Pour apple-Calvados filling into a deep glass pie dish and top with crumble mix.
7. Bake for 30 minutes at 350°F (180°C).

'Gator Bait Cheesecake

SERVES 12

Smooth and rich, you'll want to have this cheesecake and eat it too.

Directions

1. Combine graham cracker crumbs, sugar and butter, and mix well. Press into 10" (23 cm) pie plate.
2. In a food processor, combine and purée filling ingredients (except for the 'gator bait mix) until smooth.
3. Fold 'gator bait mixture into filling.
4. Pour filling into prepared crust, and bake at 350°F (180°C) for 45 minutes, rotating pan after 20 minutes.
5. While pie is baking, combine topping ingredients and set aside.
6. Remove pie from oven and add topping to hot pie. Refrigerate until ready to serve.

Crust Ingredients
1 1/2 cups graham crackers (360 mL)
1/2 cup sugar (120 mL)
1/4 lb butter (114 g)

Filling ingredients
4 eggs, beaten
1 lb soft cream cheese (500 g)
1 1/2 cups sugar (360 mL)
1 oz whipping cream (30 mL)
1/2 tsp vanilla (2.5 mL)
1/2 tsp lemon juice (1/2 tsp)
1 oz 'gator bait mix (page 113) (30 mL)

Sour Cream Topping ingredients
2 cups sour cream (480 mL)
1/4 cup honey (60 mL)
1/4 cup fresh mint, chopped (60 mL)
2 tbsp orange rind (30 mL)
1/2 cup sugar (120 mL)

Voodoo Kiss Ice Box Pie

SERVES TEN

We added a touch of mystic to our ice box pie, truly making this a pie-in-the-sky treat.

Ingredients

3 tbsp instant coffee (45 mL)

1 tbsp icing sugar (15 mL)

1/2 tsp warm water (2.5 mL)

1 1/2 cups sugar (360 mL)

1 cup water (240 mL)

10 egg yolks

Voodoo Kiss:
1/2 oz each Black Sambuca,
Bailey's Irish Cream (15 mL)

4 cups whipped cream (35% fat) (1 L)

Directions

1. Combine coffee, icing sugar, and warm water, and mix into a paste.
2. Combine sugar and water in a saucepan, over high heat. Heat to boil, and remove.
3. Beat egg yolks with whisk and mix with paste.
4. Add liqueurs and mix till thick.
5. Add slightly cooled sugar syrup and beat continually until cool.
6. Fold in thick, stiff whipped cream.
7. Pour into springform pan and freeze until set.

NOTE: Other flavourings can be substituted instead of Voodoo Kiss, such as 2 cups (480 mL) of cubed watermelon – a cool summer treat.

Drinks

Simple Syrup/108
Lemon Mix/108
Cajun Vodka or Cajun Gin/109
Cajun Martini/109
Cajun Bloody Caesar/110
Bourbon Sour/110
Mint Julip/111
Ramos Gin Fizz/111
Sazerac/112
Natchez Gin Rickey/112
Milk Punch/113
'Gator Bait Cocktail/113
Long Island Iced Tea/114
Mardi Gras/114
Monte Cristo/114
Voodoo Kiss/115
Café Noir/115
Café au Lait/115
Café Brûlot/116
Iced Tea/117
New Orleans Chicory Coffee/118

Simple Syrup

MAKES 20 OZ (600 ML)

Ingredients

10 oz sugar (300 mL)
10 oz water (300 mL)

Directions

1. Heat water, add sugar, and bring liquid to a boil.
2. Remove when sugar has completely dissolved.
3. Let cool, store in a bottle with a pour spout.

Lemon Mix

This is the mix we use for our cocktails and lemonade. We also add it to our iced teas.

Ingredients

4 parts fresh lemon juice
3 parts simple syrup

Directions

1. Combine and store in refrigerator, in a bottle with a pour spout. For lime mix use fresh lime juice.

Cajun Vodka or Gin

Directions

1. Put 4 to 5 jalapenos, seeded and sliced, into a bottle of vodka or gin and let marinate in refrigerator for at least 48 hours before serving.
2. After one week, if you haven't used the vodka or gin remove the peppers.

Ingredients

4–5 jalapeno peppers
1 bottle vodka or gin

Cajun Martini

Directions

1. Swirl vermouth in a chilled glass and discard.
2. Pour Cajun vodka or gin over lots of ice into cocktail shaker and immediately strain into a rock glass for "on the rocks," or a martini glass for "straight up."
3. Garnish as desired and drink while still cold.

Ingredients

2 oz chilled Cajun vodka or gin (60 mL)
speck of vermouth
olives or lemon with a twist

Cajun Bloody Caesar

Ingredients

1 12-oz (360-mL) glass rimmed with celery salt
1 1/2 oz Cajun vodka (45 mL)
2 shakes Worcestershire sauce
2 shakes hot sauce
5 oz Clamato juice (150 mL)
pinch of salt and pepper
ice
celery stick and a wedge of lime for garnish

Directions

1. Fill glass with ice, add Worcestershire and hot sauces, salt and pepper.
2. Pour in vodka and stir.
3. Add Clamato juice to the top of the glass and stir quickly. Garnish and serve.

For a Cajun Bloody Mary use tomato juice instead of Clamato, and garnish with a lemon wedge.

Bourbon Sour

Deceptively simple, sinfully delicious, our signature drink mixes Wild Turkey and lemon for a landslide of taste.

Ingredients

1 1/2 oz bourbon (45 mL)
3 oz lemon mix (90 mL)
ice

Directions

1. Half fill a shaker with ice.
2. Add bourbon and lemon mix.
3. Shake 25 to 30 times rigorously (up and down).
4. Pour immediately into iced glasses.

If you prefer it sweeter, add some simple syrup (page 110).

Mint Julip

This Southern cooler was extremely popular during the Plantation Era. The mint fragrance gives the drink a refreshing aroma and makes it perfect for hot summers.

Directions

1. Using a muddler, crush the mint leaves with syrup and put into the glass.
2. Fill glass with ice to the top.
3. Pour bourbon over the ice and stir swiftly.
4. Top with ice water and a dash of brandy.
5. Garnish with mint sprig and serve with a straw.

Ingredients

1 9-oz (270-mL) glass
6 mint leaves
1/2 oz simple syrup (page 108) (15 mL)
1 1/2 oz bourbon – we use Wild Turkey (45 mL)
ice
1 sprig of mint
dash of brandy

Ramos Gin Fizz

Invented in the 1880s by Henry C. Ramos in his bar at Meyer's Restaurant, this is one of New Orleans' most famous drinks. The secrets of its delightful taste and texture are orange flower water and egg whites. When Huey Long was Governor of Louisiana, he brought with him to New York's Roosevelt Hotel a bartender from New Orleans just so he could have New Orleans' gin fizzes in New York.

Directions

1. Combine all ingredients and pour over ice in shaker.
2. Shake vigorously 20 to 30 times till mixture becomes frothy and thick.
3. Pour into selected glasses – we use tall thin ones.

Ingredients

1 1/2 oz gin (45 mL)
4 drops orange flower water
1 egg white
1 oz simple syrup (page 108) (30 mL)
1/2 oz lemon mix (page 108) (15 mL)
fill shaker 3/4 full with ice

Sazerac

Named for the New Orleans bar where it was invented, the Sazerac is made with an pernod derivative, bourbon or rye whisky, sweetening, and lots of showmanship. An impressive way to coat the glass with pernod is to twirl it in the air and catch it. Recommended only on the first drink.

Ingredients

1 oz bourbon or rye whisky (30 mL)
2 drop Angostura bitters
2 drops Peychaud bitters
1 tsp simple syrup (page 108) (5 mL)
1 tsp Pernod (5 mL)
1 twist lemon peel

Directions

1. Combine all ingredients except the Pernod and lemon peel in a cocktail shaker.
2. Put the Pernod into a pre-chilled old-fashioned glass, then tilt the glass in all directions to thoroughly coat the inside with Pernod, and pour off any excess.
3. Mix the ingredients in the shaker thoroughly with a cocktail spoon – do not shake!
4. Strain into the chilled, coated glass and garnish with a twist of lemon peel.

Natchez Gin Rickey

This popular cocktail is allegedly named for Colonel Joseph Rickey (rumoured to have been a member of Congress). This drink is perfect for a sweltering summer afternoon, served in a tall glass with lots of clinking ice.

Ingredients

1 1/2 oz gin (45 mL)
2 oz lime mix (page 108) (60 mL)
2 oz cold sparkling soda (60 mL)
dash of cassis
garnish with lemon and mint sprigs
lots of ice

Directions

1. Fill shaker with ice and pour in gin and lime mix.
2. Shake 25 to 30 times and pour into selected glass (usually a long one).
3. Add soda and a dash of cassis.

Milk Punch

Milk Punch is a soothing drink — a pleasant tonic for the morning after. We love to mix it in a hand shaker until it's frothy and white, and then add a sprinkle of nutmeg on top for colour.

Directions

1. Half fill a cocktail shaker with ice.
2. Pour ingredients over ice and shake 20-25 times.
3. Pour into high ball glasses with nutmeg on top.

Ingredients

High ball glasses
1 1/2 oz bourbon (45 mL)
1 oz simple syrup (page 108) (30 mL)
1/2 tsp orange flower water (2.5 mL)
1/2 tsp vanilla extract (2.5 mL)
4 oz cream (10% fat) (120 mL)
1/2 cup crushed ice (120 mL)
ground nutmeg

'Gator Bait Cocktail

This bait may not attract any alligators, but it will entice your guests.

Directions

1. Fill shaker ¾ full with ice.
2. Pour in 1½ oz (45 mL) of liquor mix and 3 oz (90 mL) juices.
3. Shake 25 to 30 times.
4. Serve with ice in a wine glass, garnished with lemon or pineapple.

'Gator Bait Mix

Equal parts:
Blue Curraco
Midori
Irish Cream
Malibu Rum

pineapple/orange juice mix

ice

Long Island Iced Tea

This drink is a real mixed bag — vodka, tequila, triple sec, rum and gin with lemon and Coke.
This is something you'll really want to put on ice.

Ingredients

ice to fill glass
1/2 oz vodka (15 mL)
1/4 oz each of tequila, triple sec (7.5 mL)
1/2 oz each of rum, gin (15 mL)
2 oz lemon mix (page 108) (60 mL)
cola
lemon slice for garnish

Directions

1. Fill glass with ice.
2. Pour combined liquor over, and add lemon mix.
3. Top with cola and garnish.

Mardi Gras

Ingredients

1 oz bourbon (30 mL)
1/4 oz Kahlua (7.5 mL)
5 oz hot coffee (150 mL)
whipped cream and a little sugar
for topping

Directions

1. Pour hot coffee into stemmed, glass mug. Add bourbon and half of the Kahlua.
2. Top with sweetened whipped cream and the rest of the Kahlua.

Note: Try replacing the Kahlua with Grand Marnier for a Monte Cristo.

Voodoo Kiss

Directions

1. Pour the hot coffee into a special glass mug with a stem.
2. Add the Voodoo Kiss mix.
3. Top with whipped cream/sugar mix and 1 tsp of Black Sambucca.

Ingredients

1 1/4 oz Voodoo Kiss Mix (38 mL)
1 tsp Black Sambucca for drizzling on top (5 mL)
5 oz hot coffee (150 mL)
whipped cream and sugar for topping

Voodoo Kiss Mix:
equal parts Black Sambucca, Irish Cream

Café Noir

A good Creole cook never boils coffee, but drips it slowly until all the flavour is extracted. The modern drip coffee-makers that use paper filters work very well. Allow 1 rounded tablespoon (15 mL) coffee per cup (240 mL) pour in freshly boiled water, wait for the rich fragrant aroma to arise, and serve in fine china cups.

Café au Lait

This is the thick, rich coffee New Orleanians traditionally drink in enormous quantities every day, at breakfast, lunch and dinner, and at the French Market coffee houses with hot beignets.

Directions

1. Combine the milk and cream in a heavy saucepan and bring just to a boil then immediately remove the pan from the heat.
2. Using large coffee or breakfast cups or mugs, fill one-third full with hot chicory coffee.
3. Add the hot milk and cream until the cups are two-thirds full.

Ingredients

6–8 cups hot New Orleans chicory coffee (1–1.5 L)
3 cups whole milk (720 mL)
1/3–1/2 cup heavy cream (80–120 mL)

Café Brûlot

As a dramatic climax to an elegant dinner, you can serve a flaming café brûlot after dessert. The heady combination of coffee, brandy and rum, cinnamon and cloves, orange and lemon peel makes this a delicious grand finale. The ribbon of gold-blue flame follows the lemon peel spiral as the mixture is ladled in the air for dramatic effect. If you plan to do this for guests, practice the technique first. Special brûlot sets of bowls, ladles and cups are available, and are a traditional wedding gift in New Orleans. Café brûlot can also be made in a chafing dish and served in demitasse cups.

Ingredients

1 lemon

1 orange

24 whole cloves

2 cinnamon sticks

1 1/2 oz triple sec (45 mL)

1 oz brandy (30 mL)

1 1/2 cups strong black
Creole café noir (page 115) (360 mL)

Directions

1. Peel lemon with one continuous motion so the peel is in a long spiral. Peel over brûlot bowl so that any juices go into the bowl.
2. Peel the orange in the same fashion.
3. Insert the cloves into the spiraled lemon and orange peels at 1" (2.3 cm) intervals so that the peels are studded.
4. Place the cinnamon sticks, in brûlot bowl over medium-high heat.
5. Add triple sec and brandy, and stir.
6. Carefully ignite the brandy.
7. Stir, lifting the ladle high in the air – a ribbon of golden-blue follows the motion.
8. Mount the peels on a fork so that you can hold them over the brûlot bowl for flaming.
9. Ladle ignited brandy over peels.
10. Gradually add coffee, pouring around the edge of the bowl, so that a hissing sound is heard, and continue mixing until the flame dies out.
11. With a fork, squeeze small amounts of orange juice into the bowl to sweeten the coffee.
12. Pour into demitasse cups with the brûlot ladle and serve.

Iced Tea

Freshly brewed, this summertime beverage will really make a storm in your teapot.

Orange Pekoe Iced Tea

Directions

1. Let the tea bags steep for 30 minutes in the boiled water.
2. Remove and discard bags.
3. Pour tea into a large container and add cold water, lemon mix and syrup. Let cool and refrigerate.
5. Serve in pint glasses, filled with ice and garnish with lemon wedges.

Ingredients

5 tea bags
24 oz boiling water (720 mL)
24 oz cold water (720 mL)
10 oz lemon mix (page 108) (300 mL)
4 oz simple syrup (page 108) (120 mL)
ice
lemon wedges for garnish

Herbal Iced Tea

Using the same method as above, replace tea bags with any of your favourite herbal teas, such as apple spice, peppermint or camomile.

New Orleans Chicory Coffee

Traditional New Orleans coffee is a rich, very strong dark roasted blend of many different beans, mixed with roasted ground chicory root. The dark roasting and special blend of beans give the coffee its characteristic strength and bite; the chicory gives it the thickness and special flavour. The coffee made by New Orleans coffee blenders is not available elsewhere, though I have found some in Chinatown from Café du Monde. Proportions of coffee to chicory vary considerably. All you need to make good New Orleans coffee is an inexpensive 6-cup (1.5 L) Neapolitan coffee pot or the kind of drip pot available in discount stores, and paper coffee filters or paper towels cut to fit.

Ingredients

6–12 cups cold water (1.3–3 L)
1 6–cup (1.5 L) coffee pot
1 paper coffee filter
7 heaping coffee measures of chicory coffee
2–3 quarts fresh water (1–2 L)

A couple of useful suggestions: Turn off the kettle's heat once the water comes to a full boil – over-boiled water will alter the flavour of the coffee.

You can continue dripping boiled water through the same grounds until the coffee begins to look pale – the drip method in the following recipe uses a great deal of coffee but it makes it go quite a long way.

Directions

1. Set a large kettle of cold water to boil.
2. Put a coffee filter in the upper part of the pot, to cover the perforations.
3. Fill the upper part with 7 heaping coffee measures, or cup chicory coffee.
4. When the water comes to a full boil, turn off the heat and pour a small amount (about 3 tbsp (45 mL)) of the boiled water over the coffee just to dampen the grounds.
5. Wait 30 seconds.
6. Fill the upper container with boiled water and let drip through.
7. When all the water has dripped through, fill the upper container once again.
8. The bottom section will be full of coffee once you have filled the top section two or three times. Pour the coffee into cups to serve or into a coffee server set on a warming tray.

Lagniappe

Blackening Mix

MAKES 1 ⅓ CUPS (320 mL)

This mixture can be kept, in an air-tight jar for up to 3 months.

Ingredients

1/2 cup sweet paprika (120 mL)

1 1/2 tbsp salt (22 mL)

2 tbsp each onion powder, garlic powder (30 mL)

2 1/2 tbsp cayenne (38 mL)

1 1/2 tbsp each fresh ground white pepper, fresh ground black pepper (22 mL)

2 1/2 tsp each thyme, oregano, basil (12 mL)

Directions

1. Sift paprika, salt, onion and garlic powders and cayenne in a large bowl.
2. Mix all remaining ingredients until completely combined, and sift again.
3. Store blackening mix, covered tightly, in a cool place.

Bronzing Spices for Meat or Fish

MAKES 1 ⅓ CUPS (320 mL)

Bronzing is a lighter, milder form of blackening and should be done on a stainless-steel pan.

Ingredients

1/2 cup sweet paprika (120 mL)

1 1/2 tbsp salt (22 mL)

2 tbsp each onion powder, garlic powder (30 mL)

1 1/4 tbsp cayenne (18 mL)

2 1/2 tsp each freshly ground black pepper, freshly ground white pepper (13 mL)

1 1/2 tbsp thyme (22 mL)

2 tbsp each oregano and basil (30 mL)

Directions

1. Sift paprika, salt, onion powder, garlic powder and cayenne into a large bowl.
2. Mix all remaining ingredients until completely combined and sift again.
3. Cover well and store in a cool place.

Basic Mayonnaise

MAKES 1 ¼ CUPS (300 ML)

Directions

1 Combine the egg, lemon juice, salt and pepper in a food processor. Purée these ingredients for about 15 seconds and in a slow, steady stream add the olive oil.
2. When all the oil has disappeared, remove mixture from the processor, scrape the sides and then purée this mixture again.
3. Refrigerate in a sealed container at least 30 minutes before serving. This mayonnaise must be used within 24 hours.

Ingredients

1 large egg
1 tsp fresh lemon juice (5 mL)
1 tsp salt (5 mL)
2 tsp black pepper (10 mL)
1 cup olive oil (240 mL)

Crème Fraîche

MAKES 3 CUPS (720 ML)

Directions

Blend the ingredients together in a glass bowl with a rubber spatula until well combined. Let the cream sit overnight, covered with a dry cloth. Do not refrigerate for the first 24 hours.

Ingredients

2 cups whipping cream (480 mL)
1 cup buttermilk (240 mL)

Crab and Shrimp Boil Spices

Makes 8 ounces (240 mL)

One of the grandest of New Orleans' traditions is the boiled seafood dinner, featuring large platters piled high with boiled crabs, boiled shrimp, and when they're in season, boiled crawfish. On the side there may be pickled marinated crabs, pickled oysters, fried softshell crabs, fried trout and perhaps catfish and hush puppies.

This is the "bouquet garni" of spices for seafood Courtbouillons. It is used to flavour the water in which crabs, shrimp or crawfish are boiled.

Ingredients

1 cup salt (240 mL)
6 tbsp lemon juice (90 mL)
3/4 tsp Tabasco (4 mL)
1 tsp allspice (5 mL)
5 whole cloves
4 sprigs fresh thyme
1 tsp dried thyme (5 mL)
5 whole bay leaves, broken in half
1 tsp celery seed (5 mL)
1/2 tsp dry mustard (2.5 mL)
1 1/2 tsp freshly
ground black pepper (7.5 mL)

Directions

1. Combine all ingredients, mix well and store in a cool place. This boil mix will keep for about 2 months.

Marinated Black-Eyed Peas

SERVES SIX TO EIGHT

Directions

1. Soak black-eyed peas overnight in cold water.
2. Strain the peas, put into a pot of boiling water and bring to a rolling boil on high heat.
3. Turn heat to low and simmer until tender, approximately 1 hour.
4. Strain peas and mix in the remaining ingredients.
5. Allow the mixture to sit for 24 hours in the refrigerator.

Ingredients

2 cups black-eyed peas, dried (480 mL)
1/4 cup fresh dill, chopped fine (60 mL)
1/4 cup Italian parsley, chopped fine (60 mL)
3/4 cup purple onion, chopped fine (180 mL)
1/4 cup balsamic vinegar (60 mL)
1/2 cup olive oil (120 mL)
1/2 tsp salt (2.5 mL)
1/4 tsp pepper (1.25 mL)

Marinated Purple Onion

Directions

Toss together the onion slices, olive oil, vinegar, salt and pepper and let sit for at least 1 hour. We like to serve this with smoked salmon crostini (page 43).

Ingredients

1 purple onion, 1/4" (0.5 cm) slices
1/4 cup olive oil (60 mL)
2 tbsp balsamic vinegar (30 mL)
1 pinch salt
1/2 tsp black pepper (2.5 mL)

Pickled Okra

Ingredients

2/3 cups cider vinegar (160 mL)
2 tbsp salt (30 mL)
1/3 cup water (80 mL)
22–25 small fingers of okra
3 small hot peppers
1 tbsp dill seeds (15 mL)
1/2 tbsp mustard seeds (7.5 mL)
3 garlic cloves

Directions

1. Sterilize jars by placing into boiling water for about 5 minutes.
2. Remove the jars and allow to dry in a clean place.
3. Combine vinegar, salt and water and bring to a hard boil on high heat. Meanwhile, place a few fingers of okra in each jar.
4. Pour the hot vinegar mixture over the okra in the jars.
5. Allow the jars to cool, then put on lids tightly and store in a cool place for at least 1 week.

Remoulade Sauce

MAKES 4 CUPS (960 mL)

Ingredients

1 cup olive oil (240 mL)
1/2 cup vinegar (120 mL)
1 1/3 cups Creole mustard (300 mL)
1/3 cup paprika (80 mL)
1 tbsp ground black pepper (15 mL)
1 1/2 tsp salt (7.5 mL)
1/2 cup white horseradish (120 mL)
1/4 cup mayonnaise (60 mL)
3 cups celery, minced (720 mL)
2/3 cup parsley, minced (160 mL)
1/3 cup onion, minced (80 mL)
1 cup Louisiana style hot sauce (240 mL)

Directions

1. In a large mixing bowl, combine the olive oil, vinegar, mustard, paprika, pepper, salt, horseradish and mayonnaise.
2. Add the celery, parsley and onion and mix well.
3. Add the hot sauce and mix well.
4. Store covered in the refrigerator. Keeps for two to three weeks.

NOTE: Hot sauces to use are: Laredo Hot Sauce, Franks Hot Sauce, Crystal Hot Sauce or any sauce that does not contain colour or additives.

Blackening Tips

Blackening should be done either outdoors or in a commercial kitchen, because the process creates an incredible amount of smoke. A gas grill is best, as it will produce enough heat to heat the skillet to the proper level. Cast iron is the only suitable material for a blackening skillet, and it must be dry when heated.

Before you start the process, bring the meat or fish to room temperature. Then dip the food in butter and sprinkle with the blackening mix. This process creates a barrier between the food and the hot skillet to allow blackening, instead of burning, to occur. You can reduce calories by cutting out the butter. And, if you want to increase the spiciness, roll the food in blackening mix instead of sprinkling.

Keep in mind that blackening is not a suitable method for cooking beef beyond medium. Before the inside can cook to medium-well the meat surface will burn, tasting bitter and of ash, instead of being blackened, which leaves a sweet, wood-cooked flavour.

Heat the skillet over a very high heat until it is just short of forming a white ash or white spot on the bottom of the skillet. Place the meat or fish on the pan, cooking each side for 1 to 2 minutes, until done. If you want, you can finish cooking your blackened food in the oven.

After cooking, clean the skillet by burning off extra sauce. When the skillet has cooled, wipe it clean (don't use soap) and rub it with vegetable oil. Store in a dry place.

Fried Foods

There are two keys to frying foods well:

1. Use only fresh (unused) oil. The molecules in fresh oil are close together and relatively inactive. Food dropped into fresh hot oil acts like an irritant to the oil, which responds very quickly by immediately sealing the batter, and the oil then cannot get to the food inside. All crumbs, drops of batter, salt or water that fall or are released into the oil during frying separate the molecules and therefore weaken the oil's ability to seal the breading or batter. That's why you should shake off excess breading or batter before frying.

    Even frying unbattered foods (such as French fries) affects the oil's ability to seal off the outer surface of food so the inside won't be greasy. As a matter of fact, simply heating oil in the first place begins to break it down, and the more you re-heat it, the less like the original oil it is. That's why you should change your oil frequently, instead of putting oil aside to be used again.

2. According to "Louisiana Kitchen," by Paul Prudhomme, "You should use enough oil to completely submerge whatever you're frying; generally this is from ½ inch to 4 inches deep."

3. For our frying, we use peanut oil, which requires higher heat for breaking down, but you can use Canola or vegetable oil if you prefer.

How to Eat Crawfish

1. Twist the tail off the body and immediately suck the juice out of the body shell. (It's what we mean by "sucking the heads.")
2. Hold the tail by the bottom and peel off the top ring of the shell.
3. Place the meat between your teeth, pinch the bottom of the tail with your thumb and forefinger, and pull the meat out with your teeth.
4. Keep on going!

Paneed Foods

"Paneed" is New Orleans terminology for pan frying. For the best pan-fried crust on meat or fish, the oil for frying should be just deep enough to come to the sides of the food but not to cover the top. Always drain on paper towels.

Roux

A roux is a mixture of flour and oil. The cooking of flour and fat together to make roux is a process that seems to go back as long as 400 years ago. Roux can be made in a matter of minutes over very high heat. The basic reason for making a roux is for the distinctive taste and texture it lends to food.

How to Make Roux

The usual proportion of oil to flour is fifty-fifty, but always have a little extra flour. Roux can be made in advance, cooled and then stored in an air-tight jar for several days, in the refrigerator or at room temperature. If roux is made ahead, pour off excess oil from the surface and re-heat (preferred) or let it return to room temperature before using.

   Light and medium-brown roux: used in sauces or gravies for dark meats or game, giving a nutty flavour.

   Medium to dark brown roux: used in sauces and gravies for white meats such as pork, rabbit, veal, and all kinds of freshwater and saltwater fish and shellfish etouffes and gumbos.

   Black roux: is the base for our Bayou Chicken, one of our most popular dishes, and it was developed especially for this recipe. It's very difficult to make without burning so we recommend staying with the dark brown roux.

Several words of advice are essential:

1. Cooked roux is extremely hot and sticks to the skin. It's best to use a long-handled metal whisk, oven mitts and a large enough skillet.
2. Be sure you have no distractions so you can fully concentrate on making the roux.
3. If possible, use a heavy skillet with flared sides – this makes stirring easier, which makes burning the roux less likely.
4. The oil should be smoking hot before the flour is added.
5. Once the oil is heated, stir in the flour gradually and stir or whisk quickly and constantly, including scraping down the sides of the pan, to avoid burning the mixture.
6. Constantly move the pan on and off the heat until you have control of the desired colour.
7. As soon as the roux reaches the desired colour, remove it from the heat and continue stirring for 3 to 5 minutes until the mixture has cooled.

NOTE: If black specks appear in the roux as it cooks, it has burned so discard it.

Glossary

ANDOUILLE – the most popular Cajun smoked pure-pork sausage. Pronounced "ahn-doo-ee"

BAIN-MARIE – container with water in which you place another container to cook

BEIGNETS – Creole doughnuts, squares of dough deep-fried in oil with confectioners' sugar sprinkled on top

BLACKENING – meat or fish rolled in herbs and spices, seared briefly in a white-hot cast iron pan, sealing in the juices – and guess what – it's black!

BLANCH – when water comes to a boil, food is quickly dipped, cooked briefly and placed in cold water

BLEND – combining ingredients thoroughly

BOIL – to cook until liquid bubbles

BRABANT – spicy, oven-roasted new potatoes

CAYENNE – thin long hot red pepper used for seasoning, usually found in the ground form in Cajun dishes

CHICORY, CHICORY COFFEE – in New Orleans chicory coffee comes from a particular white chicory root, and is different from the chicory used as a vegetable. The chicory used in coffee is dried, roasted and ground in the same manner as coffee beans.

CHILI SAUCE – spicy tomato sauce, sweet and peppery

CLARIFIED OR DRAWN BUTTER – this is made by melting butter over very low heat. Skim off the white scum and strain the clear butter into another receptacle. Clarified butter is purer and does not burn as easily as unclarified.

COAT – to cover with a thin layer such as a flour mixture

CORN FLOUR – not to be confused with cornmeal. Corn flour is light and powdery; cornmeal is grainy.

CRAB, HARD-AND SOFTSHELL – crabs evolve from softshell crabs into hardshell crabs. They molt, lose their shells, then begin anew to grow a hard shell. In Louisiana, they are caught in either stage and cooked in a variety of ways.

CRAWFISH, CRAYFISH – a small edible crustacean. The universal local pronunciation is "crawfish" and this has become the preferred spelling. Elsewhere "crayfish" is the accepted spelling, and the word is pronounced accordingly, (in French, *ecrivisses*).

CREOLE – generally used to describe a style of cooking associated with New Orleans

CREOLE MUSTARD – distinctive locally made mustard using spicier and darker mustard seeds than average; the seeds are marinated before preparation.

CREOLE TOMATOES – preferred locally grown in New Orleans premium tomato – resembling Beefsteak or Jersey tomatoes

EGG WASH – a mixture of eggs and milk in which certain meats, fish or vegetables are dipped before frying or before dredging in flour or bread crumbs then frying

ETOUFFEE – literally it means smothered; in Louisiana cooking "etouffee" signifies covered with a liquid. It refers to a dish with a cooked roux in the etouffee sauce. (In French Louisiana we don't put the accent on the first "e" – that would mean to smother a person!)

FILE – a powder made from dried wild sassafras leaves used as a flavouring and a last minute thickening agent in one form of gumbo, gumbo file

GUMBO – gumbo is a Cajun soup almost always containing a cooked roux and sometimes thickened with okra or gumbo file; it usually contains a variety of vegetables and meats or seafood and is served over rice. Many people top their gumbo with gumbo file.

JAMBALAYA – pronounced "djum-buh-lie-ya" it is a rice dish, highly seasoned and strongly flavoured with any combination of beef, pork, smoked sausage, ham (or tasso) or seafood, and often containing tomatoes.

KNEAD – working dough by folding and stretching

LAGNIAPPE – an old Creole word (pronounced "lah-nyahp") for "something extra or special." There are lagniappes of information at the end of this book.

MARINATE – to allow food to set in a liquid mixture to tenderize or blend flavours

MINCE – chop food, generally vegetables, into very thin pieces

OKRA – vegetable popular for making gumbo and also eaten as a vegetable. Originally imported from Africa, where it is called "gombo."

ORANGE FLOWER WATER – a derivative of the orange tree blossom essential in making the authentic Ramos (New Orleans) gin fizz

PECANS – pecans are usually specified in the recipes as "dry roasted." This is important for flavour. Place shelled pecans, halved or pieced, in a large ungreased roasting pan and roast in a 425°F (218°C) oven for 10 minutes, stirring occasionally.

PEPPER – all the recipes use white and black pepper freshly ground from pepper mills. White pepper is milder than black, and invisible when ground into most food; it is therefore used for light-coloured sauces. Cayenne or red pepper is only sold already ground or in liquid form as Tabasco. It is important that the cayenne or Tabasco used in cooking be fresh.

PINCH – a small amount, usually ground seasoning (grasped between fingers)

PONTCHARTRAIN – the large lake forming New Orleans' northern boundary gives its name to a sauté of crabmeat (sometimes shrimp, too) added to enrich broiled or sautéed fish

POOR BOY – generic name for the standard New Orleans sandwich made with French bread

PRALINE – Louisiana praline is a candy patty popular in the South, made from brown sugar, nuts (especially pecans) or seeds and sometimes butter and/or cream.

RAMEKIN – an individual baking dish, 3 to 4 inches in diameter, much like a miniature souffle dish.

REDUCE – to boil liquid until part of it evaporates

REMOULADE – cool, pale sauce born in France has become in Creole hands a peppery, brick-red dressing redolent of hot mustard, scallions, parsley, lemon and cayenne, used on cold and spicy boiled shrimp or crabmeat and sometimes halved, hard-cooked eggs

RICE – the rice universally used in local dishes is long grain white rice, which cooks up fluffy and is widely available nationally.

RONDEAU – a deep-sided heavy saucepan which can be put in the oven and cooked

SIMMER – cooking on an extremely low flame

TABASCO – a nationally marketed liquid form of cayenne made from red peppers grown on Avery Island, Louisiana, and bottled by the McIlhenny Company. Tabasco and cayenne are specifically indicated in the recipes; they serve the same function but are used in different quantities and cook differently.

YAM – highly prized, locally grown strain of sweet potato. In mush of the South, the word "yam" is used interchangeably with "sweet potato"

Discography

by Richard Crouse

"Birth of the Blues," Al Hirt
    That's A Plenty, Al Hirt, Pro Jazz

"Dans Le Jumbo," Compagnie Creole
    Nos Premiers Chansons, Compagnie Creole, Saisons

"Do You Know What It Means to Miss New Orleans," Louis
    Armstrong. Pops The 1940s Small Band Sides, Louis
    Armstrong, RCA/Bluebird

"Eating and Sleeping," Earl King
    Creole Kings of New Orleans, Various Artists

"Goin' Up the Country," Barbecue Bob
    The Voice of the Blues: Bottleneck Guitar Masterpieces,
    Various Artists, Yazoo Records

"Hot Stepper's Dance Zydeco," Rockin' Sidney
    Live with the Blues, Rockin' Sidney, JSP Records

"I Used to Love Her," The Dirty Dozen Brass Band
    Voo Doo, The Dirty Dozen Brass Band, Columbia Records

"Jambalaya," Jo El Sonnier
    Cajun Spice: Dance Music from South Louisiana,
    Various Artists, Rounder Records

"Let the Good Times Roll," Shirley and Lee
    Single #3325, Alladin Records

"Lou-Easy-An-I-A," Preservation Hall Jazz Band
    New Orleans Vol. 4, Various Artists, CBS Records

"Red Beans," Professor Longhair
    Crawfish Fiesta, Professor Longhair, Alligator Records

"Second Line Medley: I Done Got Over/Iko/Iko/Hey Pocky Way,"
    Irma Thomas. Live! Simply the Best, Irma Thomas, Rounder
    Records

"She's Got Me, Hook, Line & Sinker," Smiley Lewis

"That's A Plenty," Kid Ory's Creole Jazz Band
    Good Times 1954, Kid Ory, Good Time Jazz

"Too Hot to Handle," Duke Robillard & His Pleasure Kings
    Too Hot to Handle, Duke Robillard & His Pleasure Kings,
    Rounder Records

"Zu Zu Man," Dr. John
    Zu Zu Man: 18 Classic Tracks, Dr. John, Zillion Records

Index

A bit about Robin...

Born in Scotland, Robin Grindley brought with him to Canada his lusty sense of humour and rapier wit.

He's been in the restaurant business for many years and his work with Frances goes back to her Rosedale Diner days. He left the Diner to join Frances in her new venture.

As the following for Southern Accent grew, so did Robin's commitment to his own new challenge: painting. His hidden talent, which started slow, built quickly, and it is now his full-time focus.

Working the door at Southern Accent part-time, the "Host with the Most," sells his art off the walls of Southern Accent as well as his namesake cafe, Robin's Nest Cafe.

Like his partner Frances, Robin's mind is always at work, churning out new ideas and his paintings now appear on cards and T-shirts with who-knows-what on the horizon. And of course, on certain evenings he can still be heard roaming the stairwells and hallways of Southern Accent, chatting with friends and charming strangers.